The Gospel of Joy

Global Impact of the Ministry of Joy to the World

James McReynolds
Minister of Joy to the World

The Gospel of Joy: Global Impact of the Ministry of Joy to the World
ISBN: Softcover 978-1-955581-65-3
Copyright © 2022 by James McReynolds

Parson's Porch Books is an imprint of Parson's Porch *&* Company (PP*&*C) in Cleveland, Tennessee. PP*&*C is an innovative organization which raises money by publishing books of noted authors, representing all genres. Its face and voice is **David Russell Tullock** (dtullock@parsonsporch.com).

Parson's Porch *&* Company *turns books into bread & milk* by sharing its profits with the poor.

www.parsonsporchbooks.com

The Gospel of Joy

Contents

Acknowledgments

I have dedicated this book to those who have shared joy to me and others in this life. Everything happens for a reason to those who love God and are called to God's purposes. Dr. John Killinger, my dear friend and mentor, for more than 50 years, has encouraged me in every way possible. He introduced me to Dr. David Russell Tullock, publisher for Parson's Porch Books. Tullock has created a miracle for me in that my books are read throughout the world. This message would not have been possible without Tullock and his amazing team. My first book with Parson's Porch, *The Spirituality of Joy*, was carefully edited by Eric Killinger, John's son. I opted not to gain royalties for myself, but to trust Tullock and his team as they share eternal Life by giving bread and meeting the needs of people in all creation. This is my 12th book with Parson's Porch.

God is doing miraculous things in every corner on earth. Together God delights in our sharing the eschatological bread that brings us together with one Lord, one faith, one baptism, one God and Father of us all. The bread of eternity nurtures our souls for now and forever.

I am grateful for people who allowed me to express my joy in churches and so many varied places. These kind people have enlarged my vision quests to express where only the Spirit could have made possible. The ideas in this book were first shared in sermons, classrooms, counseling sessions, and other outlets. Somehow God has allowed me to share joy throughout the world in places I never imagined.

I thank my best friend and partner, Laurel Ann McReynolds. She has endured my twelve-hour days of writing to complete my manuscripts. Her delightful insights and musings shaped my own thoughts as I wrote. We have prayed and served together as we shaped our marriage and life together. Thank you, Laurel, for your love and care and encouragement. I so love you.
Finally, I want to thank my family. My beautiful daughter Linda, who writes briefs and other works as a corporate communications lawyer in Washington, D.C. She reads my manuscripts with a keen eye of a journalist.

I thank Ethan Coffin, my grandson, to whom my first Parson's Porch book was dedicated in 2011. His artwork has enhanced the covers of each book. Ethan is now a freshman at Lafayette College in Easton, Pennsylvania. Linda and Ethan remind me of the love of God for everyone. What a joy to enjoy them now. and I love each eternally today and always.

"Everyone has a divine right to joy, love, shining bright, dreaming big, achieving your hearts' desires, and continues rebirth living life to your fullest potential. If I can, you can." -Lia Valencia Key

Dedication

This book is dedicated to all of those who during these times of another pandemic, more wars, and worldwide recession, have shared the gospel of joy, fed the hungry, served in small places, and practiced patience in all circumstances.

I dedicate this work to the girl on the cover who trusted Christ and professed her faith when I served as her pastor in Weeping Water, Nebraska. I gave her a new leather-bound Bible. I enjoyed her reading my scripture text on Sunday mornings.

What a joy to know a soul was saved through Jesus. Read I Corinthians 3:6-8.

Foreword

Jim McReynolds has done it again! He has filled another book from cover to cover with sheer, unadulterated joy. This man is a marvel. He truly is. I really believe he could be confined in a straitjacket, strapped in a briar-studded, hard, and unyielding chair in some subterranean prison with an unforgiving noise level produced by constantly thudding jackhammers and screaming air-whistles, and still think about how wonderfully joyous it all is.

Age has not dimmed his voice or quelled his spirit.

Now in his 80s, Jim is more devoted than ever to this ever-recurring theme in all his writings, that no matter how desperate our circumstances or how mitigated our pleasures, there is an indefinable, insuperable joy at the heart of human existence, and we are grossly remiss if we fail to note it and celebrate it with every heart's breath we take.

I sometimes wonder what it must be like to be Laurel McReynolds and to married to this fantastically positive and celebrate eternal joy. The illustrious Norman Vincent Peale, author of the perennially best-selling *The Power of Positive Thinking*, was right, all those years ago, when he heard Jim preach a sermon, anointed him the Minister of Joy to the World. It took one to know one, and Peale was nothing if he was not the great drum major of joyful, creative thinking from his pulpit on Fifth Avenue in New York City. Perhaps Laurel, who has served Jim's meals and helped to keep his house or what now proved years on end.

Perhaps one day she would favor us with a book of her own, or at least an article, in which she describes what it has been like to share a home with this irrepressible genius of the eternal joyful attitude. Laurel is a joy herself, reflecting in her personality and face the supernal glow from her love for God who gives eternal joy.

In 2019, Jim announced and sought to establish a National Day of Joy at the end of each month of June. What better way could we or the world around us to be reminded of the importance of this all-affecting human emotion, so that, for a while at least, there is a fire lit in the darkness of people's souls a glowing lamp of hope, and, given a few years to spread and grow, it can turn into an international festivity of new awareness, annually transforming our sad, old world into a whole new Garden of Eden?

Jim is correct. We must adjust our vision, our vey way of viewing the world, so that we regard it, not sadly or mournfully, as so many do, but joyously and excitedly, the way it must have been greeted by Adam and Eve at the birth of everything that has come to be.

He is also right in thoughtfully preparing this book to be released in the wake of the great pandemic, the dampening, disparaging shadow of the Covid virus that has fallen across our entire globe in recent years. How sad many of us have become. How dreadfully we rise in the morning and plod through our restrictive days, hardly daring to hope for a normal future in the time ahead. We are dwelling like galley slaves, almost too weary to ply our care in these dark waters of disease and loneliness.

This is not who we really are. This is not what we were made for. It is not the stage upon which we were meant to act out our varied parts and characters. Jim has forcefully reminded us; this is not the way life should be.

God has not set us in the world to be glum and afraid, pulling long faces and thinking how terrible it all is. With the joy from God, we climb the highest mountains and sail the deepest sea, laughing ad yodeling our way through everything until we have tamed the sprawling wilderness and transformed the most disparaging jungles the most delightful spas.

It is difficult to do justice, in a mere foreword, to the spirit that has authored this book for such a time as the one through which we presently pass. Jim, we are once more in your debt for the way you have shared your beautiful, shining spirit with those of us whose hearts have flagged and whose hopes have dimmed, even if not fully into darkness.

Once more, you have lit a bright and wonderful lamp and set it aglow during our shadowy oppressions. We owe you, and owe you big, and we hope you will yet be given many years to dwell among us as God's unflagging guru of joy and heart-warming anticipation.

Dr. John Killinger
Warrenton, Virginia

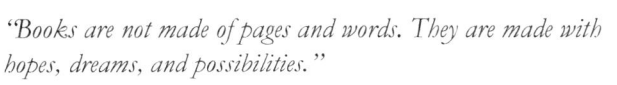

"Books are not made of pages and words. They are made with hopes, dreams, and possibilities."

--Dr. James McReynolds on his ministry of sharing joy with the world

Chapter One

Living in Joy

Joy is the good mood of the soul. Brené Brown writes that there is something soulful about joy. She defines joy as an intense feeling of deep spiritual connection. (Brené Brown, *Atlas of the Heart*, pp. 205-206) How does a person live with joy? Experiences of joy are difficult to articulate. When I encountered a serious study of the emotion joy, I thought I had missed it. As I walked along on the Vanderbilt University campus, I listen to the song of a bird, the breeze was softly blowing. I stop to look at the blueness of the sky. I breathe deeply and speak "Thank you" to God for letting me live in such beauty. I know I was filled with delight and gratitude, but I could not explain it.

"If joy is a product of seeing that there is meaning and goodness in life, then why isn't our joy more full? Why is it limited to a few occasions when some particularly touching occurrence affects us at the depths? Why can't we live in joy?

"Life was made for joy, and there's an eternity in every instant of it." (John Killinger. *For God's Sake, Be Human*, p.150)

In my quiet time, I listed things that bring me joy. This pursuit of joy brought satisfying and contentment as I reflected with the students in a class on joy. I found that the deepest moments of joy take me completely by surprise.

Joy moves us so quickly that a cascade of other experiences show up. We may that why can't this feeling last forever. Joy is often fleeting. One night when I was with my family in the Anza-Borrego State Park in Southern California, I walked outside to the place we took our trash. I was in a hurry to get back inside. I then caught a glimpse of the sky. I stopped and looked up. Dazzlingly beautiful. All was quiet and still. Standing there for some awesome moments, I gazed at the cloud formations layered in red and baby spanked pink hues ahead of the coming night.

Joy comes a surprise. We are taken off guard for the moment from our spiritual, mental, physical, and emotional routines. This joy is not just for a lucky few. It is a choice that anyone can make. If joy is a choice, how do we make it? We cultivate the emotions that we want to experience. This requires a commitment to conscious thought. It takes awareness of how we handle external events of our living moments. Reactivity alone doesn't nurture joy. Activities that are performed repetitively changes the structure of our brain.

Change the way you talk to yourself. Self-talk reflects your beliefs. Watch it and be aware. Those things you are telling yourself are either moving you closer to possibilities of joy, or further away. Learn to follow your bliss. Adults learn "to put away childish things." The ability and desire to express our deeper selves does not extinguish.

Everything happens for a reason. Everything that happens to us has meaning for our lives. People live through incredibly difficult events. We then miraculously discovered meaning in what they lived. Amazing how it sounds, it is, "All things work together for our good." Everything is connected. I was born in Holston Valley Hospital in Kingsport, Tennessee. The physician who delivered me was a graduate of Carson-Newman College and the University of Tennessee Medical School. Born on a Tuesday, my parents enrolled me in the cradle roll at First Baptist Church in Kingsport the following Sunday.

I eventually chose to attend Carson-Newman, a Baptist Christian university. My two brothers attended the University of Tennessee in Knoxville. My brother Edward graduated from the University of Tennessee Medical School. Everything happens for a reason.

Every child of God could list the perceived highs and lows of life. We need to have a sense that there is purpose and value to everything. When you discover the meaning of events of your life . . . your birth, where you attended school, who you married, who taught and encouraged you, the use of your gifts . . . everything changes. We feel stronger because this vision of the best you is a source for confidence. We are more in touch with who we are. No matter the weather at the surface of the ocean, the depths are undisturbed. That is how I understand joy.

Becoming right with ourselves makes us right with the world. Joy helps us understand, forgive, empathize, and harmonize the conflicts of living.

Knowing that there is a reason for what happens to us saves us from a blaming perspective. Nobody is to blame. Everyone is responsible. Blame is like an Australian boomerang that loops around and hits us on the head. The only way to look at life is to restore the reality that there is a good reason for everything. That is how George Bernard Shaw understood it. "This is the true joy of my life, the being used for a purpose recognized by yourself as a mighty one, the being a force in nature instead of a feverish, selfish clod of ailments and grievances complaining that the world will not devote itself to making you happy."

Everyone has the right to joy, love, shining bright, dreaming big, achieving the soul's desires, and to continuously rebirth life to the fullest potential. Joy creates more joy. Worry attracts worry Joy attracts joy. Talking about our problems is a habit that must be replaced by talking about our joys. William Blake expressed it in the poem "Eternity." "He who binds to himself a joy does the winged life destroy, but who kisses the joy as it flies lives in eternity's sunrise."

We long for the steady grace of everyday joy-filled intimacy. It is never too late to recover it. Union and communion are available to use. Joy comes from the love of God where no strings are attached. We become kind and compassionate to each one we encounter. A passenger on an airplane flight as if we will change seats because the window seat throws her into a panic. We politely oblige. Kindness is life-giving. Each opportunity brings us more joy.

To be intimate with Jesus, we still the noise within us. Daily living becomes invitations, appeals, and challenges from the Holy Spirit to our spirit. A chance meeting with a stranger on a plane invites a sharing more intimate than a person with a close friend, a parent, or a spouse. We must recover the discipline of letting ordinary persons and events invite us to see deep meaning. The faces of joy are as diverse as the stars. Each is unique as a snowflake.

I want to be an inspiration. No matter what my faith and understanding of the past, I need to leave it behind. My spouse Laurel and I spend time trying to put pieces of challenging jigsaw puzzles together. In life's puzzles, we come to realize that the life puzzles cannot be put together as they might have been. No matter how insignificant we feel, we can make an impact. Nobody but God can be everything to everybody. Most people will make it clear that they have found the reason for living in joy is the result of someone cared enough to listen, to be kind in a world that has no capacity to become an inspiration.

I have studied joy and joyful people for half a century. Joy requires discipline. Travels throughout the world and the writings on my research and books on the emotion joy has given me insight on what people in joy do. Joyful people abide in Christ, continuing to be intimate with God. Joyful people read. Reading the Bible is an incredible source of joy. Read Psalm 19:8, 119:14, 162. Joyful people celebrate. They drop everything to rejoice in the good things in life. Joyful people sing. Singing releases the joy in the soul. Read Ephesians 5:18-19. Joyful people meditate. Read Psalm 63:5-7. Joy does not forget to remember and thank God. Joyful people give. Read II Corinthians 8:1-2. The generous spirit is a joyful spirit. Joyful people serve. Read Psalm 100:2. Joyful people hope. The most joyful think about heaven. The vertical focus on heaven is their highest hope. Joy is more than earthly pleasure. Joy is enjoyment of God. Joyful people know their destination will not be entering heaven but entering eternal joy. Read Matthew 25:21.

Frederick Buechner, a Presbyterian minister who does more writing than preaching, wrote a novel named *Godric*. In his wisdom, he wrote, "All the death that ever was, set next to life, would scarcely fill a cup." When our thoughts turn toward heaven, we perceive the big picture. Death is puny compared to the vastness of life.

In my sermon celebrating my brother David's death, I comforted his family and friends with saying that David was going to place where there will be no goodbyes. There will be the joy of one long hello. Read Revelation 21:4.

James said, "Count it all joy." James 1:2. The spiritual life is a journey into the fullness of joy. Joy is as complete as the love between Jesus and God his Father. Read II Corinthians 8:2. The Holy Spirit is our guide and comforter. Across the years, when life's perplexities impoverish us, the Holy Spirit working through the gift of joy, removes all boundaries to our hope. Joy is found in unusual places.

The key is acceptance. Everything happens for a reason. Accept the miraculous way pain and life events have molded us. When we accept life as it is, we become more dependent on our maker. The past cannot keep us from joy. Release and relief are possible. Everything happens for a reason. Living in this world is a mystery. We feel ill at ease because living here is not ultimately what we were created for. We were made for heaven. Everyone will continue to be restless until we reach our heavenly destination. Remember the hymn that has been sung for ages, "Turn your eyes upon Jesus. Look full in his wonderful face. And the things of earth will grow strangely dim in the light of his glory and grace."

Choose to hope as you decide to not be stuck in a rut composed of numbness, anger, sadness, unwise spending, and emptiness. Blame less. Bless more. Love more. Be kinder. Doubt less. Dream more. Discourage less. Encourage more. Gripe less. Cheer more. Sit less. Move more. Joy will cover your being. Joy replaces the feeling of being unsatisfied and insignificant. One secret to my own joy is focusing on what God tells me, not what the world throws toward me. Practice saying "no" to things you need to let go of. Say "yes" to the things that will make your life better. Saying "no" will help us refocus on what gives joy. Have the courage to begin now with the endurance to keep going. J.R.R. Tolkien wrote, "I have found Joy in small things. We find joy and peace within ourselves is life's ultimate gift for us. In today's world, it is a challenge." Everyday deeds keep darkness away with simple acts of kindness and love.

Simple acts of kindness will make someone's day. Find your passion and create a life in which each day is a meaningful, enjoyable experience. Planning long term goals is unavoidable. Visualization helps define us as humans. Joy surrounds us when we celebrate the small achievements. Little time is needed when we smile at someone as they cross a road. Take time to take somebody's groceries to their car. Celebrate and appreciate those moments. Long term goals will be sustained. Enjoy your quiet time with the Holy Spirit. Enjoy a cup of tea or coffee. Try solving a crossword puzzle. Read something inspiring. Each drop of water makes an ocean.

In our moments of disappointment and sadness, we want somebody to hold us close. Some cannot tolerate their negative feelings. I know I have been disappointed by those who did not show up for me. I could spend time to make a list of bosses, situations, minister who are now bishops, directors of synods or presbyteries. They bypassed me and my feelings. They judge us. We react by turning their dismissal into another useless story about brokenness. Striking back at them through self-destructive moments. It is then difficult to have compassion. That person's insensitivity is often entirely about them and their emotional discomfort. Set boundaries. Adjust your level of attachment.

Their cruel response may be for the moment. Maybe they have been there for you for many years. Expand your compassion for yourself and for others experiencing the journey with you. Trees around our old house were cut down when we decided to build a new home. We had to remove the stumps and the roots. The roots continued to grow to the point of clogging up our neighbor's drain pipes. I think of those roots as like the dynamics of our relationship with others and God. Most of us have metaphorical trees that have been cut down, but the roots are still growing beneath the surface. These old roots must be completely removed. These roots are established and deep. Our ministries of bringing joy to our relationships, our churches, and the whole world. We must work together to focus our attention to eradicate the toxic root systems that cause us "to miss the mark."

We live in the shadows and in darkness. We are involved in pride, racism, and other sins that fester and grow in hiddenness. The light from the joy of God brings clarity, exposing the places and situations where we have been deceived. Read Matthew 5:14. We must become agents in the world sent on a mission or vision quest to shine the light of Jesus.

Since 2019, I have celebrated the National Day of Joy on the last Wednesdays in June. The purpose of all my praying, preaching, teaching, and writing is to inspire and encourage people to experience joy and share this delight with others. Nine out of ten of the people I ask believe the world needs more joy. The joy of our salvation requires a genuine commitment to promoting joy and inspiring others to make the world a more joyful place.

I asked residents of the Good Samaritan Care Center in Syracuse, the South Lake Care Center in Lincoln, and the Louisville Care Center in Louisville, Nebraska what triggered the most joy for them. Family dinners brought them the most joy. Other activities they shared were listening to a favorite song. Spending time outside. Receiving a hug from a loved one or a friend. Watching a favorite television show or a movie. Spending time with family. Reading. Talking walks. Learning to use technology.

The pursuit of joy is often relegated to the background of our lives in day-to-day responsibilities. The activities shared by care centers in Nebraska does not take much energy or time. No matter your age, finding and sharing joy will brighten the day and improve physical, mental, and spiritual health.

Living Out the Gospel

Most of the people I have asked distinctly to agree that the world needs more joy. Half of them say friends bring them joy. They highly agree that the world does not have as much joy as it used to. Talking to family brings joy. They say that surrounding yourself with positive people fosters the energy. If I have learned one thing, it is that even in difficult times humans hold the capacity to experience joy and to spread joy to others. I wholeheartedly agree that celebrating moments of joy each day is the best thing we can accomplish. Joy is living out the simple gospel. It is now our time to live out the gospel.

The fractures in our foundation are not beyond repair. Imagine what things would happen if the church linked arms across cities and denominational lines and ministered on the things that need changing.

The only way to experience joy is to do what you have a passion and talent for doing. Keep your eyes on the goal. Don't miss the blessings on the way. Living in joy is to live a life you are proud to life. Make a list of the most important aspects of your life. Being busy is not the same as being productive. Our compassion and kindness give us balance. Joy-filled people hug the hopeless. Comfort the grieving.

Laugh with those who rarely laugh. Life is full of challenges and opportunities. Grasp courage with both hands. The joy of making an impact is priceless.

Eternal joy is not out there, but here and now. Joy and the fruit of being joined with the Spirit and seeds that are matured in our lives now. God created us like God and doing and sharing this fruit impacts eternity at the root of our being.

Living in joy, as the world defines joy is a pale imitation of the joy that only God can give us. If things are going well, that is joy. Joyless souls feel burned out, lied to, cheated on, scammed, and robbed. When events become difficult, there is no joy. Joy is an integral part of the kingdom. Read Romans 14:17. Ministers of joy know that living in joy involves doing the will of God. The writer of III John experienced the joy of ministry. Read III John 1:4. Inner joy is never taken away. Joy is strengthened when we remember that as Peter did. Read I Peter 4:13. When we grieve the Holy Spirit by our sin, we interfere with the flow of joy. Eternal joy stays as we reevaluate our relationship with God in Christ. Joy is the uncommon quality associated with Christian living. Jonathan Edwards listed signposts to separate genuine religious experience from its fakes, the Puritan minister looked for evidence of joy. (Jonathan Edwards, *Religious Affections*, pp. 104-105, 248253, 262-265) Paul Tillich wrote of joy as the quality of life we experience when we restore ourselves to who we are. (Paul Tillich, "The Meaning of Joy," *The New Being*, p. 146) Tillich wrote, "Joy is nothing else than the awareness of our being fulfilled in our true being, in our personal center." (*Ibid.*, p. 146)

Joy comes from filling the spiritual void with supportive relationships, primarily an intimate relationship with the pure joy of Jesus. Joy is the strong foundation that supports a healthy life. To grow in joy, we resist self-pity. We are not self-centered. For joy to flourish, we focus on loving others, and especially loving God.

Add gratitude. Humility. Forgiveness. Faith. Hope. Patience. Love. Subtract fear. Worry. Anger. Greed. Materialism. Jealousy. Pride. Complaining. This results in flourishing joy. God is more joyful than any human ever was. God is in delightful anticipation of many new "sons of God."

Living in joy includes living in sorrow. Read about godly sorrow in II Corinthians 7:10. Joyful people frequently experience godly sorrow. People who feel the worst about feeling guilt, anger, anxiety, and fear from their sinning feel joy in the amazing grace of God. Suffering is limited to our short life timelines. Read Romans 5:2.

"Joy, we think, is spontaneous but has little staying power. Joy cannot sustain us over in the long haul. But the joy we receive as Christians is not that of a passing occasion. Rather it is a joy that derives from finding our true home among a people who carry the words and skills of God's kingdom of peace." (Stanley Hauerwas, *The Peaceable Kingdom: A Primer in Christian Ethics*, p. 147)

Some things reveal more soul than others.

Stones participate in being. Plants are alive. Animals are higher beings. They live and have being and sensing. Human beings add reasoning. We share in the life of God more fully than any other creature. Reason is like intuition. Prayer involves amazement. Knowledge is no longer a possession. There is a change from lordship to fellowship. Prayer brings a miraculous and complete union that is beyond imagination. Read Psalm 62 and Habakkuk 2.

A life of prayer connects what we say with what we do. False connections are broken. New life is created. Our souls are made and re-made into mystery and surprise. I experience God. God experiences me. I experience what I am like in the mind of God. I know myself trough the mirror of the love of God. Read Isaiah 43:1. In prayer, I hear God's whisperings as if in a quiet gallery. Saint Paul's Cathedral in London was not constructed as a whispering gallery. Worshipers discovered it. God whispers to those who belong to the Divine lover. God assures and repeats reassurances as if in a whispering gallery. Read Ephesians 1:4-6.

Wonder is the joy of identification. Humans experience wonder when they seek to open themselves to God and others. Prayer, gratitude, and joy provide the foundation from which we move away from self. Prayer is the grace by which we open ourselves to that which is not me in the present moment. Intimacy with God through prayer shows how God's limiting is the definition of love. Nothing can separate us from this love. When a person reaches the desirable state of pure love, and tries not to, that one can do nothing but love and be joyful. Joy is the echo of God's living in us. Jack Gilbert described "the stubbornness to accept our gladness in the ruthless furnace of this world." "Words for Grief," *The Christian Century*, March 9, 2022, p. 6.

Joy anchors itself deeply into our being and stays. Establishes roots. Endures all circumstances. Raises consciousness. Most have a limited view of the possibilities of a life of joy. Imbedded into these thoughts is that we can live a better life on earth if we seek God. Read John 10:10. Life often appears grim and sad. Christians must learn to enjoy themselves. There is joy in heaven, and there is joy on earth as we receive foretastes of joyful eternity in the gifts that God gives us.

Joy dazzles us, surprises us. Joy is to be had not in the future, but now. The apostle Paul could claim objectivity about his advice to rejoice always. Read I Corinthians 12:4-11. Joy happened in real history. His joy had historical facts behind it. Paul's descriptions of joy had its source beyond mere earthly human joy. Joy could not be destroyed by outward circumstances. This delight was found in unusual places.

Threats to joy are not obvious.

Souls are deprived by denigrating, by advancing the belief that joy is not important to survival. We must consider the universal right to joy. Without joy, life and liberty, health, and safety, are not essential. Joylessness is no life at all. It is mere existence. Joy brings existence into living. Christians might go on missions or vision quests not just to alleviate physical suffering, but to bring comfort through music, beauty, and humor.

Visitors who travel to a nation that is joyless feel the cramped living, the greyness of the inner cities, lack of fresh water that constrains joy. We ooze out tips for possible joy. Joy can color perspective. Joy initiates spirals that can take us upward to well-being. When leaders of nations invite us to share things like teaching the English language deep down, they want help from despair. I fully realize that I cannot fix everyone or everything. Trying to be in control entangles us in a web of frustration and confusion. I am not a self-appointed Holy Spirit for the world. God handles everything better than I could ever could. That brings a peace that is beyond my understanding.

Making your home a house of joy

When we designed our new custom-built home, we placed a lovely stain glass art piece between the office and the bedroom. It changes colors throughout the day.
Our office faces Elmwood Park. We enjoy seeing the sun rise each morning. Laurel enjoys her music room with her piano, harp, books, and music. She allows the sounds of music to keep her calm. Listening to music or playing her piano always improves the mood of everybody in our home.

Our home is to us like the mansion mentioned in the Bible. Heaven is not just "a place out there." Eternity starts now. Eternity is a relationship. It is the intimate communion in love and freedom between us and God.

I usually drink a glass of water at breakfast with a yogurt. I eat creative bread. I try to watch my diet. Being healthily fed as my day begins is priceless. We enjoy our home. However, we need to get outside, even in the Nebraska cold winters. Walking outdoors, even just to look in the mailbox boosts our energy. Joy should not be postponed. Joy enables us to deal with the stress of living.

Pauline Chen offers an ultimate test for the joy of living. The ultimate setbacks and disappointments of living are minor in comparison to the joys. Knowing the good and the bad shaped your status in life. Being reconciled to all. Gathering the real-life treasures. Laughing as a measure of the quality of life. Letting go and just swimming away. Having no unfinished business. Creating joy not only in your life, but in the lives of other people. Loving God with all your heart, mind, and soul. Loving others as you love yourself. Experience a peace beyond understanding. Being prepared for the final ending. These are the subjects for your final living examination. (Pauline Chen, *Final Exam: A Surgeon's Reflections on Morality*, pp. 209-210)

In an appendix for this book, I will share some questions I have used in using psychotherapy and coaching in leading people to find joy amidst the frustrations of the setbacks and challenges. After some sessions of counseling, times of listening to my preaching, Times of stepping back and focusing on the experience of joy.

Joy brings on internal contentment. Sensitive seekers believe that everything happens for a reason. Reaching success after many struggles ignites joy. Joyful people experience joy moments that far outnumber negative times. My writing has given my anointed words exposure throughout the world. Only by googling "books by James E. McReynolds did I happily realized that my main publisher in the past ten years, Parson's Porch Books, has enabled the "joy of the Lord" to reach inhabitants throughout the world. I volunteered to give up my rights to royalties.

David Tullock, a kindred soul, has realized his calling is focused upon publishing books. He is enabled to turn his profits into bread as he meets needs of the poor and needy throughout the world.

My personal vision quest has helped in my annual and lifetime goals. Only with miraculous gifts from the Holy Spirit do I find joy in the journey. Some of my books have been translated into many languages. Letters of gratitude fill my collections of joys. I do not need money as I have lived beyond the biblical three score and ten years. Whether God grants me six more days, six months, or six more years, I am delighted at my adventures for the rest of my life.

I have too many likes and dislikes. Friends and family have enabled me to understand what joy looks like. In my journal in quiet times of intimacy with God, I write the goals I desire to accomplish. I reflect on the joys that I have already experienced. I focus on things that make me feel rewarded and valued.

I now have more physical and mental difficulties. I am faithful to continuous evaluation from my physicians. I follow their instructions to a tee. The word "salvation" includes "salvos," which means healing. Joy in living comes as we realize that we deserve mental, emotional, and spiritual health and the joys you are gifted with by the grace of God.

Imagine the Rest of Your Life

Imagine the future. Go to your quiet place. Clear your mind of the fears and frustrations of the day. Forget about family drama. Forget your chores. Forget health issues during this intimate prayer time. Focus on the years you have left remaining. Focus on a future that is filled with surprises of joy. Focus on what creates that joy. Write down what you visualize. Refer to this self-examination as a reminder to keep on track for finding more joy in your journey.

Redirect your thoughts. God knows we will have some bad days. Everything happens for a reason. Accidents. Injuries. Crises. Mistakes. Failures. Rejections. We are never immune. The only thing we have any control over is how we react to everything that happens. Old age is like a bank account. We withdraw from it that we have put in. Deposit kindness and joy into the bank account of memories. A 100-year-old Lutheran minister, who lived at the Good Samaritan Center in Syracuse, Nebraska, gave an effective sermon for the residents of the care center.
His suggestions were to give me, expect less, free your heart from hatred, free your mind from worries, and live simply. He used Philippians 4:8 as his text. He had chosen to dwell on lovely, praiseworthy, and excellent things.

In the mirror of mercy, our eyes of faith cut through dense underbrush of doubt to a clear vision. We experience in our limit's new possibilities. Those who are being saved are "little words" within God's Word as models of faith, hope, and love.

Our thinking influences every aspect of life. Lasting change and optimism are preceded by changed thinking. No area of living is untouched by your thoughts. Our own outlooks would change if we would decide to love like the old Lutheran minister. He had served in small churches such as the Lutheran church in Otoe, Nebraska.

Reframe negative events into learning experiences. By changing your thoughts, difficult times can become growth opportunities. Slow down. We need not rush through life. Stop to notice the delightful wonders of life. To find joy in the journey, spend your money on experiences that cause you to feel alive. Pay for things that produce joyful memories for you. Travel and gain cultural knowledge. When I traveled to China in 1986, I realized how much Chinese people love their children. James C. McReynolds, a cousin from New Jersey, took scores of trips to Saint Petersburg in Russia. I shared much valued time at the theological seminary in Saint Petersburg, called an academy, as the journey brought understanding and hope. During the Cold War, both Russians and Americans discredited one another in their propaganda designed to cause us to hate each other.

Some joy jumpstarting is realized as we attend concerts and museums. We are never too old to learn a new language. We can always get a renewing hobby. Surround yourself with joyful people who have positive connections. Dr. John Killinger, my major professor at Vanderbilt University Divinity School, introduced me to Parson's Porch Books as a possible publisher. John's talented son Eric was the editor for my first Parson's Porch book, *The Spirituality of Joy*. John Killinger has published at least 90 books and he knows the realities of publishing. He also knows the long struggles of conversion.

"There are basically two quite different kinds of conversion. In one kind the rejected aspects of our inner being emerged and are integrated into what we are and have been," wrote Morton Kelsey. We must juxtapose the future and the here and now as one reality. The reality is that God sent Jesus into this world to save humankind. Read Galatians 4:4. God gave us salvation while we were yet sinners. Read Romans 5:8. Now is the decisive moment of salvation. Read II Corinthians 6:2. All creation waits for the hour of full redemption. Read Romans 6:3-11. The resurrection of Jesus gives us the first fruit of God's promise. The Holy Spirit dwelling inside us assures us now of our future life as we are faithful and loving now. We do not have an "immortal soul," but we do have an intimate relationship with God which we accept or reject while we are still living.

Eternal life belongs only to God. Our faith is in a living, loving, saving God. Our future is rooted in the present. Read John 5:24. Humans are given time to mature the spiritual seed. Out of our acceptance of God's salvation out of love, we will do the fruit of the Spirit. Doing these deeds of kindness and goodness are to save us but are the natural characteristics of those who have received salvation. Our deeds are shown by obedience to our conscience, our compassion to our fellow creatures, our loving while we are being hated, and continuing to love and forgive despite how hopeless this appears to the forgiver. Our love rooted in God transcends time and space. We reflect God's image and likeness. We become sons and daughters of God, and we share in the eternal who is God. We become "the other Christs," whose lives will be perfected. The Gospel of Joy shows us now how to begin eternal life.

"In another, there is simply a turning upside down of the personality, with the former life being buried securely in the unconscious and the unconscious coming to the surface. People become rigidly righteous, as they were thoroughly dissipated and angry as before." (Morton Kelsey, *Companions on the Inner Way*, p. 192) For me the ministry of writing this book was my gospel of joy. Writing is a special labor of love. To me writing is play. Joy ought to be goal for our age, and the hope of each year in the next centuries. Focus on the present day at hand. Writing has taught me about this process. When I slack off and write infrequently, my writing is no longer tight and focused. I must keep organizing my notes. I edit and I rewrite again and again. I restore my desires and discipline. I make a commitment.

After we journey through this life, we will all end up in a funeral place or some mortuary. Except for pastors, it is unimaginable to most people. I held my breath the first time I visited in a funeral home. There was no smell at all. It is the least spooky place you could imagine. There is no life there. After 70 years of ministry, I am not squeamish. I am used to life and death. Most bodies do not resemble the person who lived in it. Skin changes color. Faces change.

Dying is not always the worst thing. Living a long life and suffering in old age is the terrible fate that waits for many of us. We pray that those caring for us are kind, empathetic, and full of love.

"We often say that nothing lasts forever. That's true as far as we mean that our lives and all that is around us are transitory. But there is One whose Kingdom, power, and glory do last forever." (Adam Hamilton, *The Lord's Prayer: The Meaning and Power of the Prayer Jesus Taught*, p. 138)

The soul is rich when it is content, and it is always content when its desires are fixed on God. Nothing can bring greater joy that doing the will of God for the love of God. Blissful joy Christ Jesus promised to us for eternity. The knowledge that heaven awaits is reason for joy. Read Revelation 7:15-17.

Unsinkable Faith

My readers, parishioners, counselees, and friends, I want to give you a toast. May you join you in the communion of the saints and obey their wise counsel. Accept the challenge of joy as it never fades.

Our visions of what the future looks like can be gone in an instant. We may feel as if we are stuck in a whirlpool, slowing being pulled under, but longing for joy. Storms slam into our reality. Peace and joy rush back as we invite God in. Intimate prayer and scripture equip us to navigate the stormy seas. Souls anchored in God will not sink.

Letting go of things that weigh us down releases negativity. Living in joy will not be smooth sailing. Whirlpools will not be avoided on the voyage. Pope Francis gave his apostolic exhortation on *The Joy of the Gospel* in 2013.

"The joy of the gospel fills the hearts and lives of all who encounter Jesus. Those who accept his offer of salvation are set free from sin, sorrow, inner emptiness, and loneliness. With Christ joy is constantly being born anew. I wish to encourage the Christian faithful to embark upon a new chapter of evangelization marked by this joy, while pointing out new paths for the church's journey in years to come." Pope Francis, *Evangelii Gaudium: The Joy of the Gospel*, p. 1.

Evangelism is much like Nebraska farming. God controls the harvest. There are principles which good farmers use, and lesser farmers refuse or choose not to use. Wish farmers will out-produce less-skilled ones. Through Jesus, God is bringing a life harvest. God is calling us to live intimately as family who participate in divine life.

"If you suddenly and unexpectantly feel joy, don't hesitate. Give into it . . . whatever it is, don't be afraid of its plenty. Joy is not made to be a crumb." --Mary Oliver

Chapter Two

Vision and Joy

Living your vision is moving your life into God's plan for you. Write your book, paint your painting, build your home, live the vision. Knowing that your dream is a reality, and a possibility, is as intimidating as walking the Appalachian trail. If we have not found God in the world, we will not find God in heaven. Heaven is not some other world where we escape. The kingdom of God is already in us. If we are enjoying ourselves, we say that we are now in heaven. Heaven is the most misunderstood word in all theology. We "see through a glass darkly." When Jesus sent out 70 disciples to carry the gospel of joy to nearby towns, he tells them "To rejoice and be glad, for your reward is great in heaven." The person who chooses to live in grace already lives in heaven. Read Luke 17.

Heaven is here and now. Everything that happens to us has a reason. We all experience moments of truth where we have a choice to act in self-interest or in concerns for others. Jesus recognized that poverty is a condition of every human. Read John 12:8. That does not mean we can ignore the poor. That vision is clear that when we meet the needs of others, we make Jesus present in the world. We must see the face of God everywhere. God is with us in our physical lifetimes. A circle is a good symbol of a vision quest of the circle-sun and the circle-host which feels us with delight. Life has no beginning and no end.

Imagine. Earth is like a single cell among trillions in each human body. Whenever we open our eyes and our souls and see that God is present. The miracle is that we move beyond our darkness that prevents us from seeing that heaven is within our reach.

Touching heaven brings infinite joy.

Jesus never said that he was bringing happiness, but he used the word "joy." Joy is an aftermath. It comes after we have made a connection. The word "happiness" is defined as contentment. Favored by fortune. Gladness. Pleasure. Delight. Happiness must be earned. Joy is different. Joy is on a differing plane. Joy gives exultant satisfaction. As we experience joy, we know it. Joy comes when a baby is born. When we fall in love. When I finished writing a book. Joy is linked to something bigger than we can visualize. Joy is a sign of God in you. Joy is closely connected with love.

We need to clarify our vision. The Spirit in us enables seekers to visualize in small things, so we may be transformed to be inwardly free. We fully envision that we were once a community of lost sinners in need of forgiveness and now a community of saints swimming in a sea of compassion. People who are filled with joy live with life's inevitable limits without a complaining attitude. They are willing to change any course of action that detracts from the freedom in intimacy with God.

Joy is a paradox.

Jesus teaches us that we were created to have joy because joy is linked to heaven. Joy is the connection with the eternal. We can only know the joy connection through our earthly bodies and in this world. The difficult and human conditions force us to find new meaning for living here and now.

Our faith gives us mysterious and incredible understanding of God. God cannot be localized somewhere in space but is within our reach. When we awaken from our earthly journey, we will be held with the same arms that have always held us. We shall recognize the elusive, kind, faithful friend whose mysterious presence puzzled us.

The world needs joy. Joy is the eternal peace of knowing eternity from which warm joy wells. Helen Keller said, "Joy is the holy fire that keeps our purpose warm and our intelligence aglow." Joy is a magnetic force. Following God's plan for us and doing what brings you joy makes your vision quest become reality. Feed your vision quest the nutrients it needs to thrive and come alive.

Soren Kierkegaard wrote, "Every human being comes to earth with sealed orders." He was suggesting that every person has a hidden intention on the journey. Detours steer us toward necessary events and experiences. Detours include periods of waiting. Thwarted plans. Shooting through the eyes. Anticipation. Surprises. Every life is braided in luminous moments. (Paula D'Arcy, *Waking Up to This Day*, pp. 90-93)

Vision comes from within. Our vision. Shows us how to navigate the areas of our thoughts, feelings, and emotions. Sight is the ability to see the physical world. Vision is the gift of seeing beyond it. Sight takes the physical world in so we can participate in it with knowledge. Sight brings pleasure through our eyes. Sight is sensing control, allowing to see what is coming, which way we are going. We see how another is feeling by the expressions in the face.

Vision becomes our way of seeing. Vision comes from within. We see things that are not yet realized in the world. As we age, even those with perfect eyesight will lose acuity. His loss is replaced with inner vision. Our life journey cannot be traced on a map. Joy happens, regardless of the circumstances. Joy moves our souls from within.

Surprise is the chief character in joy. Life is full of surprises for everyone such as a rainbow after a rainstorm, an unexpected phone call from a friend. Life also includes unhappy surprises like black mold in the basement, unusual rises in property taxes, or an illness. Read Jeremiah 15:18.

During one of our trips to London, my wife and I stumbled upon a classy bookstore called Hatchard's. We marveled at the five-story building with an impressive wooden staircase. A saleswoman helped Laurel peruse the music, cooking, and novels sections. They told us that Hatchard's had been selling books from throughout the world since 1797. We were quite surprised to see a couple of my published books on the shelves. The creaky floorboards of tat building have supported the written word for eight generations. The bookstore's longevity is credited by their incredible ways of finding books to sell. They have a perfect location. A charming facility. A dedicated staff. The audacity to keep moving forward. Hatchard's stands out. This English bookstore is an exception in a world that favors excessive, single use production.

During Christmas holidays in 2021, we had the rare joy of having all our families together in our Elmwood, Nebraska home. Everyone traveling from San Diego, Bethesda, Minneapolis, and far off places needed to wash their dirty clothing. Our relative new washer conked out. With all the demand, we had to buy a new washing machine. Most washing machines last ten years. Much of the things we buy are built to fail. Some capitalist businesses call it "planned obsolescence." Products are built to fail. They cannot be repaired. They require updates. We must buy a new computer every four or five years. Everything has a set lifespan. Read Isaiah 46:3-4.

If you have a smart phone or any mobile phone, you have had to go to a store for an update. That was a "planned obsolescence." Not only do you buy an upgraded phone, but you must also purchase a new charger and adapter to go with it. The fashion industry is built around what is currently in style.

Advertisers convince us that those clothes we purchased are now outdated. Women and their male observers enjoy wearing cut up denim jeans that show sexy legs, dainty feet, and parts of private parts. This mindset infects everything we care about. Spouses. Relationships. Faith communities. Health. Home. Land. Schools. We all want beautiful, new, and classy things to spring forth fresh new lives. We want our lifespan to be filled with meaningful, impactful work.

We cannot have a Hatchard's longevity while moving at a Hardee's pace. We keep on running at warp speed with an insatiable hunger for immediate results. People want meaning and connection, but they will not take the time to build the foundation that will make a relationship last.

When couples begin to attend a new church but can be quickly out the door with the least dissatisfaction.

Enter a simpler way of living by unhurrying your soul. This is our clue to step into a more satisfying and sustainable place. The crumbling of the modern world calls to reevaluate our understanding of the will of God. Belief in God guarantees that everything will work out for the best. God assures good outlooks. It is never easy to see our lives unfolding according to a heavenly plan. Moments of joy and healing are experienced despite earthly darkness. Gifts are given. Something new is offered. This is the gospel of joy. This Good News strengthens our conviction that the unfathomable fidelity is promised. We must seek the One whose word is a promise of presence.

My departed grandmother used to say in her colorful East Tennessee voice, "We came in naked as a jaybird. We will go out as naked as a jaybird."

Proverbs teaches that without vision we perish. Being relatively unknown or anonymous does not seem to ignite a vision. Yet, this is where we can depend on God. We learn to lean on God. We defer to the dream of God. Here, in the community of obscurity in the eyes of the world, fresh desires have possibility for a miracle. A calling from God may be invisible but it is vital. We all have chapters in our lives when our visible fruitfulness is pruned back. Our strength becomes dormant. Our abilities become unnoticed by the watching world.

The world would not be the same without all seven and a half billion souls living now. Together we are better than the sum of our parts. Nebraska experienced an unprecedented flood a few years ago. National and international news showed the images of people healing guide water-soaked animals to higher ground. Churches sent money. People brought food and clothing to those who had lost everything including their farms and homes.

I am now old enough to remember the episodes of Perry Mason. I wrote down a quote from the show during an evening watch at Carson-Newman. "If this crazy world is not becoming unglued, we have all to face our need for one another."

This vision is of the kingdom of heaven where people will be kind and treat others as they themselves would want to be treated. We are unaware of what is inside of us. Without vision we never realize amazing talents. Life blinds us to the treasure buried inside. Often, we never realize the treasures we have buried. We do visualize our incompleteness and lack of fulfillment.

The love of God lies beyond human understanding. Comprehending love is beyond human words. God's love is rooted in an abiding commitment to do what is best for us. God continues to work on our behalf. Never thwarted. Never diminished. God's love draws us back into divine loving arms. Love changes the core of our being. Love overwhelms our selfishness. Love purifies our motivation. Love acts to benefit others.

Nothing shows this more clearly than when we go through tough times. Those moments turn out to have meaning because we discovered buried treasure within ourselves. We find a talent we never realized we had. We go through rough times, but we come away with something valuable. Read II Corinthians 3:18.

What calling or talent would be yours? Maybe you can write well. Enjoy artistic talent. Handle money well. Compassion. Kind. Talent for business. Solving problems. Winning clients. Each person's quest is different. We are bigger than our life circumstances. We intuitively feel and believe that we are special. Every story of an ordeal has a discovery of treasure within beyond what we could ever imagine.

Helen Keller's story is like that. She was deaf and blind in an era when there was not much understanding of either condition. She came to deal with the silence and darkness. Her talents would never have come to light if she had not struggled.

Let us be honest. Life is not fair. Some appear to live charmed lives. Others live with nothing but misfortune. Every loss can become an opportunity. Life itself submerges our talent. No loss is a total loss. We can see that something valuable and meaningful is still there. Discovery of a hidden challenge can restore joy. Finding it might save your life. Our emotional lives can be saved. There is always hope and energy to go on.

Our vision is too small. We lack the idea about which talents are most important. The word talent means that in a miraculous way we just know things without having to learn them. The reason for some challenging event is for us to find a hidden talent. Believe and trust that there are people who will recognize your talent. Look carefully at the bad things that happen. If we are fortunate to discover that the meaning of what happened to us is that we have something far more to offer than we ever imagined.

Never settle for counterfeit joy. Something big must happen in life to show us that there is surprising and miraculous joy. Crises shake us out of our blindness, deafness, and fear. Deep down we are hungry for the real thing. Read James 1:17.

Life makes things happen to show us important and vital values. Lessons can come from anywhere. No one can create a new past. We can reflect on the past to insure a differing future. Vision your life so that if you do in the future what you wish you had done in the past.

Joy is richest and most long lasting when we focus on being ourselves and doing and discovering the beauty of vulnerability and freedom from comparison. Embrace who God created you to be to make it possible for others to be themselves. I believe it was John Wesley who said, "I will do the best I can with what I have, where I am, with who I live, for Jesus' sake today." To decide to be yourself is a radical choice for people have experienced nothing but pure hell. Somebody said, "What doesn't kill you makes you stronger." The reason for our joylessness in trying to be strong is that an ordeal or loss only gave them some specific strength. Keeping on gives us strength to continue in the next steps. Today, I do things that I am called and naturally gifted to do. I preach, teach, write, and counsel with delightful joy. God's opinion of me is the only one that matters.
God created me for a purpose. I never get away from myself for even one second. If I do not like myself, I am destined for a miserable life.

Relax and be who you are.

To love myself is to accept the unconditional love of God. I then can see me as God sees me. Read I Peter 2:9. Other people may not understand or accept your uniqueness, but God does. That is all it matters. Read John 13:34-35 and Matthew 22:37-39.

The Gospel of Joy is the power of God. I have experienced God's love for me. I share this with others. People are desperate for authentic love. Love is not a feeling. Loving the way God loves means loving when there is nothing in it for me. Hurting and lonely people are hungry for the Word of God.

Imagine how the world would be if everyone would be kind, grateful, and joyful. Put a smile on someone's face. Compliment somebody. Open a door. Listen.

Until we find a way to discover the meaning of events in our lives, we cannot trust ourselves or our future. We become paralyzed. The way to know that the events are bringing forth "the fruit of the Spirit, including joy," is to evaluate our needs. Did we need an opportunity to strengthen self-confidence? We are hungry to have something in our lives that we are good at doing. We need to move forward from that which is still blocking you from the joy of living.

Our vision quest needs a foundation, a springboard. The designer and builder of our new home built a strong concrete foundation under our house. Our life foundation must be restored. That's the reason things happen to us. They involve an eternal now and future. Developing a joy-filled life is a life-ong process. People who are age eighty or more are still picking up missing pieces in their human development. Life comes to your aid just when you need it.

When we think of all the things we are attempting to do now and all the things that are important for us to do in our time left, it takes a broad foundation. Foundation strengths are the seeds to living in joy. Connect the dots. The bad event gave you strength you needed in your foundation to make it possible what is wonderful in your life right now. That negative event gave you the strength needed in your foundation to make possible the next delightful thing in your life.

Never give up. Dream and envision your dream. Make it happen. Insight without change is like an engagement without a marriage. It is windup but not delivery. Insight is never a cure by itself. We must turn a new vision into a new and better life. Only change changes things.

The will of God has been the theme of your vision quest for a long time. If you continue to miss it, have you fully committed yourself? Were you consistent? Did you continue to envision so your body, soul, and mind feel as if your vision quest was already fulfilled? There may be too many people in your life who do not want you to get what you desire. Thought generates its own energy. Some people in everyone's life does not want us to succeed. People believe that your success takes something away from them. Those are the very ones who create a field of resistance that holds you back.

When some people walk into your life, the air feels heavy. Positive energy is not flowing from them. If you want joy and miracles for your life, you must surround yourself with people of high energetic vibration that sincerely want to best for you. Super charge your desires by making use of "the joy of the Lord" inside those who have positive thoughts about you and your aspirations. These chosen people overflow with giving life-changing spiritual lessons and timeless wisdom. They will give you a road map towards joy. These spiritual teachers understand the sacred connection between the head and the heart, the inner and the outer, the soul and the body. In our own vision quest, we discover clarity, understanding, and direction. We find the missing pieces, the energy of blocking a human's reticence to living in joy. Visualize in the small things we enjoy in life. This vision keeps us from losing the spark that makes life worth living. Imagine a rose moist with morning dew. See it glistening in the morning light. Behold the fragile yet perfect rosebuds. Smell its fragrance. Imagine filming the bud blooming in slow motion. Petals unfold as the lustrous roses of many colors blossom. Read Matthew 6:25-29.

Let us treat with love that which is fragile. Enjoy the splendid vision of a world transformed by God's redemption. Our thirst for God is becoming just as great as God's thirst is for us. Nothing less than the restoration of our likeness to God. In our restoration we are disfigured by sin. There are miles to go before e reach the place grace has prepared for us from eternity. With a song in our soul and a smile on our face, we approach the door of heaven.

Loving When Experiencing Success

Living a successful life means to own a home, to have money in the bank, acquiring an education, having power more than others, having worldwide fame, raising successful children and grandchildren. Rather than accepting these definitions of success, think about how God defines success. Read Proverbs 3:3-4. Success does not come from perseverance and hard work. Love and faithfulness are the core of enduring success. Everything else fades away, falls apart, and does not matter.

Accept and cherish the endless love of God. God equips and inspires us to love others and to make us more like You. When it is difficult to love myself, we remember the awesome love that we will finally understand when we live with you.

In group, family, and even individual psychotherapy, a small poetic piece published and copyrighted by Portia Nelson has often been helpful.

"I walk down the street.
There is a deep hole in the sidewalk.
I fall in.
I am lost.
I am hopeless
It isn't my fault.
It takes forever to find a way out.

"I walk down the same street.
There is a deep hole in the sidewalk.
I pretend I don't see it.
I fall in again.
I can't believe I am in the same place.
But it isn't my fault.
It still takes a long time to get out.

"I walk down the same street
There is a deep hole in the sidewalk.
I see it is there.
I still fall in. It's a habit.
My eyes are open.
I know where I am. It is my fault.
I get out immediately.

"I walk down the same street.
There is a deep hole in the sidewalk.
I walk around it

"I walk down another street."
(Portia Nelson, *Autobiography in Five Short Chapters*)

As our vision widens, we begin to see the world and everything in it, I a fresh new way. This fresh vision is a sure sign that we are moving into intimacy with God.

Expressing gratitude to God for the gifts.

The greeting in the Russian Orthodox church is, "My joy. Christ is risen." We are never alone, we adopted daughters and sons share in the eternal community of love. Each step on our journey to joy draws us into intimate prayer. Read my book on the joy of prayer. Our commitment to treasure everything from small signs of divine goodness to the whole world is complete thanksgiving. We remember God more often than when we breathe. Read Ephesians 5:20 and I Thessalonians 5:17. Whether we realize it or not, we have begun to pray always.

Saint Francis of Assisi is the patron saint of the Methodists. We have had a statue in our lawn for more than 25 years. I relish his saying, "God has first had to do a work in you, so that God may occasionally do or say anything through you."

My vision quest is that deepening our joy is a never-ending process. Walk in the pace of grace. Be patient in a posture of receptivity to each opportunity God unwraps. As we wait in reverence, we do not worry about our future happenings. The past is gone. The present is now. The future is in the hands of God. Miracles are unfolding at our feet.

The joy of living is enhanced when we wait, when we let go of those shoulds, oughts, nevers of rigid control and learn to flow with grace. God and we are like the ebb and flow of a river as we listen for the still, small voice and we gain the wisdom of surrender. At low points, words appear to be useless, a wordless exchange unites us to the Spirit. Silence is the deepest form of listening. Despite our zeal for God, we must be patient. Noting will be revealed all at one time. We may mistake the voice of God for our own, but at least we are attempting to listen. Solitude is the way of God announcing the silent splendor of the shared treasure of the ordinary.

Is your vision big enough?

Our world is in need for people who bless everything passing. They are epiphanic messengers from whom comes every worthwhile gift. Read James

1:17. God gave me a vision that seemed too big. I want to bring joy to every single person on earth. This vision quest sounds impossible. Something like this would be impossible without the Holy Spirit. Read Ephesians 3:20. God's ways are beyond my imagination. God's dreams for me are much bigger than my dreams. God uses other people to fulfill our vision quests. There is no limit to the number of people we can reach with an international impact.

To accomplish this, we must rely on the Holy Spirit. The Spirit can bring strength. Read II Corinthians 1:3. God is the God of all comfort. God opens the door for us to be intimate with the Spirit. God sent the Holy Spirit to be our friend.

My encounter with Jesus leaves a trace in me. He can give me guidance on how to move forward to the future and what is worthy and anchored in Christ. Let this book wrap God's love around you like a cozy blanket, blessing your life and filling your heart.

Chapter Three

Salvation and Joy

Jesus clearly taught that joy is the emotion felt in heaven. C.S. Lewis said that joy is the atmosphere in heaven. Jesus promises his joy. Read John 15:11, 16:24, 17:13. For traditional Christians, the fate of the soul after death is the biggest question of life. There are several biblical understandings of salvation. In the Old Testament book of Job, he was never concerned about life after death. His desire was to feel all right again. He wanted to experience the joy he had once found in life. That was enough for Job. Job could not imagine anything else.

Have we lost the joy of salvation? Joy is shown in your face. During my ministry of bringing joy to the world, I have encountered rough and used up people who look much older than years. What does our face reveal about our joy?

Do you remember the feeling of joy when you first gave your life to Jesus? Your joy may have waned, but it is still in you. In my global visionquests for joy, I share how we can live in the joy of salvation every day. Read Psalm 51:12.

People who experience "the joy of the Lord as strength," do not live in the past. Walking in joy is remembering where you came from, but not repeating it. Read I Peter 1:8.

We forget what God has done. We do not trust in all God will do in God's own way and time. When we count our blessings, joy comes. Think of the things that God has brought you out of.

Think about what Jesus meant when he said that he is the vine, and we are the branches. Stay connected to the vine. Salvation in our time has evolved from all of history. The word "salvation" has meant differing things to the women and men in the cultures that preceded our own. Survival was their goal. They wanted to continue to exist Everybody was constantly living in fear of their enemies, disease, war, and natural disasters. They just wanted enough crops, protection afforded by fortunate alliances, and the admiration, if not actual fear, of one's neighbors. Enemies would lay waste to whole towns. Mysterious diseases decimated the population of entire nations in days or weeks. Survival was the basic need of humankind for centuries.

Joy in the Process of Salvation

Read Philippians 2:12-13. When scripture uses the word "salvation," it communicates in three tenses, past, present, and future. It shares a past event of all who have believed in Jesus as Lord. Read Ephesians 2:8. This verse speaks of an event that has occurred.

There is a present tense, as in "we are being saved." Read I Corinthians 1:18. This verse is speaking of salvation in the present tense. All who are in Christ are actively being saved from the world that is perishing. Salvation is an evolving concept.

There is also a future tense. Read Romans 13:11. Salvation meant personal forgiveness. In the gospel of John, salvation from sin was rewarded with eternal life. Read John 3:15-16. The invitation to eternal life is given again and again in John.

Remember the question in Acts 16:25-34, "What must I do to be saved?" For Paul, salvation meant literally being in Christ. Being in Christ determined Paul's life work. Paul saw the world as the flesh and was inferior to the soul and spirit. In John Killinger's inspiring book on salvation, he views Paul's writings a rationale for salvation--all have sinned. Paul gives the means— Christ died for our sins. The appeal of salvation is that it is a gift from God. Paul gives the results that God puts God's Spirit within us to live restoring and transforming lives. He gives the rules or guidelines as living in hope, humility, and love. The outcome for salvation is that God will crush the evil one and redeem the saved.

C.S. Lewis (1898-1963) wrote in *Surprised by Joy* how God closed in on him while he rode on the top of a double-decker bus on his way to the University of Oxford, where he taught. He felt a strange sensation of being enclosed in stiff clothing. Suddenly he realized that he had a free choice. He could remain stuck, or he could burst out and become a new man. Alone in his quiet room at Magdalen College, he felt God inside of him. Salvation for Lewis had been a slow process. He said he was unable to resist God.

Most people know the joy of salvation gradually. They might be raised in an atmosphere where they have no need for a dramatic long conversion.

43

Consider the fact that there was not even standardization of the correct New Testament until the year 200 A.D. Christians used texts they liked as the basis of their theology and what they believed. Hugh Wamble, professor of church history at Midwestern Baptist Theological Seminary in Kansas City, Missouri enabled his students to better understand the history of the theologies of salvation.

God's Work in Us

Salvation is not about humankind's work for God. It is able God's work in us.

Read Isaiah 64:6. The joy of salvation is a miraculous work of God. Read Ephesians 2:8-9. God's working in us for salvation is ongoing. Read Philippians 1:6.

When we married, couples became united. What am I doing today? We are "working out" our marriage day by day. Each day we are both learning and growing. We talk. Laugh. Enjoy. Unite. Experience joy in extraordinary ways. Keep working with God in the process of salvation and experience "the joy of the Lord." The kingdom of God is not just a heaven beyond the stars. It is the joy of each moment.

Joy in the Proof of Salvation

Our lives should reflect Jesus. Professing to follow Jesus, nobody is shocked when we share our salvation saga with others. Examine yourself. Read John 4:12. If we abide in Christ, we will love one another as proof of knowing the love of God in the needy world. We are not called to sit here and wait for heaven. Commitment to the Word of God is big proof of our salvation. My prayer today is that we will surrender to God and live in the joy of our salvation that is found in Jesus. When we do what God placed us here to do, joy flows through. Remember that joy is a process like salvation.

I cannot prove salvation. I can only challenge my readers and hearers with a choice. "Choose this day whom you will serve." We must decide not so much what is real but decide to choose reality. That is a matter of choice. We might choose a nightmare.

For my evangelism course at Midwestern Baptist Theological Seminary in Kansas City, I wrote a paper on "The Joy Seeker: The Joy of Our

Conversion." The theme of the discussion was I Peter 1:3-8. With this and other scripture I attempted to define evangelism's goal Read James 2:19, Psalm 51:13, Acts 15:3. More about the nature of conversion can be found in I Peter 1:3, John 3:3, Jeremiah 24:7, Ezekiel 36:26-27, and Psalm 22:9-10. In that day, Midwestern Seminary students took their Bible regardless of the name of the class. The biblical languages of Hebrew and Greek were required.

I attempted to share the effect of our conversion. I used I Peter 1:8, I John 2:29, 4:7, 5:1, 5:4. Joy is first and foremost the enjoyment of God. Read I Peter 4:12-13. Our conversion banishes the delights and pleasures centered in our sin. The joy of the Lord surpasses them. I quoted and continue to quote C.S. Lewis who wrote, "There is no other way to the happiness for which were made. If you want to get warm you must stand near the fire. If you want to get wet, you must get into the water. If you want joy, power, peace, eternal life, you must get close to, or even into, the thing that has them. They are not the sort of prize which God could, if God would choose, hand out to everyone. They are a great fountain of energy and beauty spurting up at the very center of reality. If you are close to it. The spray will wet you. If you are not, you will remain dry."

Conversion is the process of finding joy. Saved people do not get upset with others or express a bad word about anyone. The sun shines out of their faces when they talk, and it is obvious that they are living in the spirit of God.

Dr. John Killinger asked me to write about the changing shape of salvation. He sought the opinions of quite a few ministers. I had no iron-clad definitions to share. "I struggle with my own faith, and whenever I try to define it, the definition eludes me. Salvation is about freedom, sometimes passionate, sometimes a frightening freedom." I did try to express the truth that organized religion often crimps or destroys this freedom. Killinger used our initials to identify those ministers who contributed to his book. All these ministers were grateful for the protection that allowed them to be honest. I wrote, "The more detailed the instructions get, the more restrictive they are, and the more humanly created they are rather than Godgiven. There is a road ahead, sometimes clear, often ill-defined. Some seeking salvation make it like an organized group tour, what it is really means is a pilgrimage, a journey to explore unknown territory. Jesus is not a tour guide but a strong companion for the journey. Salvation does not really bring answers, it brings a new set of questions." *Ibid.*, p. 95.

Ordinary things create extraordinary joy.

When was the last time you felt an unfettered moment of joy? What did that joy feel like in your soul? Who are you when you are your most joyful self? Did reading my books on joy prompt you to seek it? These questions would be much better than the ones church people ask, such as, "If you were to die tonight, would you go to heaven? Are you saved? Do you faithfully attend church services?" These methods are disjointed and do not have a biblical or psychological foundation that makes any sense.

Phenomenologically, joy feels light and bright. Colors appear more vivid. Physical movements become more fluid. Smiles are impossible to suppress. Joy involves a state of positive effect. In a joy moment, people report experiences of safety, freedom, and contentment. Conversion broadens the perception on human suffering. Disappointments and suffering become ripe with the possibilities for the inevitable and eventual grace of God. Joy attunes us to opportunities to witness restoration and redemption of life's difficult situations. Joy helps one see her circumstances in a new light. A grateful person potentiates experiences of joy.

The first time I experienced any scholarly and most comprehensive study on the emotion joy. Dr. Christopher M. Meadows conducted a study when I was earning my doctorate at Vanderbilt University Divinity School. He had completed his Doctor of Philosophy degree at Princeton University on the emotion joy. He elicited and sorted through thousands of accounts of joyful experience from 333 university students.

Dr. Meadows' research eventually established the dimensions of a joy experience. He concluded that excited joy is extremely intense. It involves high energy. He contrasted excited joy with serene joy. Serene joy is quieter and calmer. Serene joy gives feelings of harmony and unity. His work bridges the tension between other dominant accounts of joy. Joy is inherently excited joy.

The human body aims at equilibrium with serene joy. This involves free activation. This means one readily engages with any new, stimulating, flourishing activity. Serene joy is not a withdrawn state of being. It is one in which one is prepared to engage. By allowing the forms of joy arranged from excited to serene. Serene joy aims at salvation, restoration, equilibrium. I asked him how his research could enable an understanding of conversion. I recall we disagreed, and Meadows refused to discuss it.

Another dimension of Meadows' research on joy was identified as individuated joy and affiliative joy. I still have my recordings and notes, and I wrote that individuated joy is joy experienced by an individual. In contrast, affiliative joy is. joy that is shared with others. I note that Dr. Meadows found that 70 per cent of the experiences revealed in his research were affiliative. Note that 30 per cent were individuated. Joy brings about a special bonding.

Another part of the research was identified with anticipative joy and consummatory joy. Anticipative joy occurs when the fulfillment of a desire appears to be imminent. Consummatory joy happens when the desire has already been filled. In my class notes, I wrote that consummatory joy is evidenced by a good event happened, or that some distress has been removed.

Dr. Meadows identified five characteristics of enjoying joy. He cited harmony and unity. This dimension involves a sense of internal harmony or integration within the self, as well as a sense of harmony with others.

Vitality is involved in excited joy. This is a keen sense of energy, potency, and aliveness. His research also indicated that serene joy brings more vitality than in any other emotional experience. I like John Killinger's definition of salvation: "Salvation does involve integration, self-realization, recovery of a lost order, or the complete reconfiguration of one's being. Salvation is being so totally transformed that one naturally loves everyone and everything, wishes no one any harm, and desires the radical transformation of the whole world and the universe, so it may all enjoy the ecstasy one is experiencing in oneself." *Ibid*, p. 106.

Transcendence described the content of consciousness when one is in a joyful moment. A person senses that she is moving, or has moved, soared, and passed beyond ordinary existence. During a joy experience, she feels she has transcendence bounded space and time, her past, her ordinary self-consciousness, and her ego boundaries.

Joy includes the experience of physical freedom. She enjoys freedom of thought and the freedom of thought. Biblical scholars and theologians have discovered a tight connection between joy and the sense of physical freedom.

David is described in II Samuel 6:12-14 as so overcome by his joy in the Lord that he spontaneously leaps and dances in public. He does not care that he was wearing improper clothing. The Greek word for "leaping with joy" is used in Luke 1:41-43, 6:22-23 to describe how the fetus of John the Baptist leapt for joy in the womb when he encountered the pregnant Mary. Also, as Dr. Meadows mentioned, there is a kind of epistemic freedom in joy, where one feels free in their thinking.

During experiences of joy moments, sensory perception is altered such that individuals experience heightened awareness of depth, color, touch, feeling, taste, and sound. Excited joy brings brighter sensations. The perception of time is altered. In anticipatory joy, the arrival of anything longed for is felt as imminent. Time flies in intense joy. Time passes slowly in a serene joy.

Joy and ecstasy are different. As this research indicates intense joy involves such a high degree of transcendence of the self, that one loses the cognitive aspect of joy moments. Ecstasy or bliss wipes us out. Joy causes us to be more intensely ourselves. In ecstasy, self is cleaved from the body. Ecstasy figures an escape from bodily consciousness or even of life itself, even though the body remains as residue.

Kenneth Woodward, religion editor for *Newsweek*, wrote that he often disagreed with evangelical Christians because they sponsor a conservative kind of religion that really does not conserve much of the Christian tradition. Woodward praised Dorothy Day and Thomas Merton for their remarkable spiritual journeys. He remarked about Billy Graham that he traveled constantly, but never traveled anywhere as a genuine pilgrim. Graham could not understand salvation as a process. He was already saved and so had nothing to learn from others that was of any importance in his relationship with God. *Ibid*, pp. 97-98.

Spreading the gospel of joy requires honesty in the way humans experience the world. Being saved is the first step of a long journey. Differing churches emphasize conversion. Popular means of evangelism become exclusive. Street corner preachers preach with a mind to rescue I have respect for them. If they preach with love and power, miracles take place. That first profession of faith can become a masquerade that keeps us infantile. Unless we become child-like we will not move on to a mature faith. Soul saving has to do with removing our masks to set us free. Salvation is enjoying the life of God.

My own profession of faith in Jesus came at age eight. I know it was real. Mine was incomplete and unfinished as is true of any child conversion. I was converted through other people's witness. My family and my Sunday School teachers were in my beginning. My pastor was quite evangelical. During a Vacation Bible School. The passion of that vision was set on fire, and the flame never died.

The joy of salvation comes in unique ways. I treasure my evangelical Baptist roots. Now I find friends in many denominations and traditions. Each group needs to listen to each other, if the witness of Christians is to grow in unity with integrity. Conversion is not a once and for all time event. We confuse our first profession with the lifelong process. Seekers of faith ask how they can become a Christian and remain a Christian. The process involves participation, imitation, and discipline. We are not required to duplicate anyone else's experience. In the Bible we see a wide range of experiences. Everything that happened to Christ happens to us. Converts share in the life of Christ and the records of the first apostles helps us understand our own. The Bible is vital to salvation. It is the architect of our thoughts.

Finding Joy in Christ Is Not Automatic.

Popular evangelism appears to give easily digestible solutions. This witness does not reorder the personality or sees any need for restoration. Some weak and timid person, especially young children, become narrow-minded. Conversion requires a long time to be totally saved. God's unconditional love is sure and secure.

Our actions must be in concert with our prayers. We should pray for the joy of the Lord and then we are to take the kind of actions that will enable us to find eternal joy in God. Salvation life is supernatural but not enchanted. God never magically gives us joy. God will not bring joy from what is not the gift of God or anything that is distanced from grace such as our idols of work, sports, leisure, sex. Joy comes in the same sense that fruit comes from a tree. We plant ourselves in te rich soil of the Word of God, soak in the living water of God, and bask in the sunshine of grace.

Knowledge of God and knowledge of the self cannot be separated. Sinners know that they are loved, and they weep and repent of sins. It is fatal to interpret salvation as a program for self-improvement. Believers are always making new beginnings. Souls are made and remade all the time. Conversion can focus on "my conversion." This emphasis causes us to think we are "the favored few," or the "elect." The experience is more like a love affair. It holds out risks. Pains. Joys. Soul development is the working of the Holy Spirit to restore it after the image of God.

Love is another way to discuss conversion.

The early disciples continued to learn what love is. Humans go from childhood to youth to adults. Puberty is a crisis. It is not unlike the crisis associated with conversion. Youth are in a transmission period of changing and develop personal identity. Youth are dying to the old type of living, and they wait for the new to be experienced. It is not a wonder that teenagers will "go down the aisle" or become concerted in a mass at church camps, youth revivals, or summer Bible schools.

Guided by mature Christians, lives are turned around and relationships are healed.
Like the first disciples, they hear stories. They follow Jesus. They share miracles. They share in the fellowship of a lively community. Saint Teresa of Avila experience conversion when she was 39 years of age. She had tried for years to experience Christ. She revealed that she was reading Saint Augustine's *Confessions*. She suddenly burst into tears as she had a vision of the wounded
Christ. "I threw myself down before him with the greatest outpouring of tears."

In some ways, my intense studies on joy with Dr. Chris Meadows zeroed in on God's calling for me to share the joy of the Lord with the world. I have never been exposed to so much material on any subject in my seminary days. I was so transformed that I was not surprised when Norman Vincent Peale anointed me the Minister of Joy to the World.

Chapter Four

Restoration and Joy

In my book, *How We Got Our Denominations*, I discuss the history of the Christian Church (Disciples of Christ) as part of the Restoration Movement. Read Psalm 51:12. This Christian group's goal was to get all the various denominations to join as one.

Perhaps this restoration goal comes from complete longing and desperation to restore the joy of God's salvation. The writer of this Psalm was David. He had waked away from God. He needed restoration. The psalm is a desperate request for help. David was no longer joyful, glad, and thankful for salvation. He felt guilty, anxious, and deeply depressed. Sin had made a big wall between him and God. David is pleading and begging God for restoration of God's salvation.

David was restored. He became a man after God's heart. We cannot run to the corners to hide, but we must reach out to God and ask God to restore the joy of our salvation. Jesus is the joy. Jesus is our means for salvation.

There is urgency and desperation in this plea. Sin entangles easily. We need a willing spirit to sustain us. We can never be restored to the joy of God if the spirit we hold inside us is not willing to leave the old self out. The Holy Spirit keeps us in check, renewing our joy day by day. Restoration is not to frighten us. The joy we receive as we weep, makes it possible for us to move on. We are not only restored to seeing our poverty toward God, but we also see how much we are loved. We are given ways and means of growing in discipleship. To be restored is to be receptive and available in love to anything that happens to us.

Restoration is a complete transformation of our souls. We are called to enjoy the life of God. The joy of salvation is in complete unity in unimaginable diversity. It is not just an individual happening. We discover that in identifying with the ever-widening circle of the whole, we own immense and infinite resources.

We need to repent of our divisive nature. It is easy for ministers of joy, kindness, and light to preach one thing and live another way. We expect deliverance and continue with temptations. We acknowledge our wealth and ignore poverty. We keep on straddling the fence and blaming the past. We harbor hate and pretend acceptance. We risk so little and want too much. We increase the problem and denying our part. We are undone by the power of our sins. We pursue empty enticements. "The better to seduce you with my dear," cries the temptress.

Restoration requires the unmistakable touch of grace. Every event we experience and every person we meet shows us that there are no coincidences. Everything happens for a reason. The joy of grace transformed and restored my life and lives of others. Madeleine L'Engle said, "There is nothing so secular that it cannot be sacred, and that is one of the deepest messages of the incarnation." J. G. Woititz, *Struggle for Intimacy*, pp. 155-164)

Spirituality is about relationships with ourselves, with other people, and with God. Spirituality is powerful, yet subtle. It's like breathing. If we stop, we die. It is vast and difficult to imagine. As we learn various ways of conceptualizing our spiritual journey in differing ways, involves catharsis, examination, and personality change.

Salvation has roots.

To be uprooted from the Holy Spirit is to become unhinged. The Holy Spirit is not limited. Infinite. Incomprehensible. Eternal. Our roots in salvation continue to be in mystery. Mystery is an invitation and a good seduction of the mind. We are allowed to go deeper and deeper never finishing or coming to an end. Joy and miracles happen in mystery. Salvation is rooted in aliveness, attention, and spiritual energy. Read I Corinthians 2:7, 4:1. We sink our roots in salvation and the mystery of God. Any human being without roots becomes the prey to human opinion, emotional reaction, and to do whatever is the current vogue. Restoring the joy of our salvation requires reestablishing roots. Nobody can give what one does not possess. Christianity and salvation by faith comes with the fire that Christ came to light. If anybody is not aflame with holy fire, there will be no radiation of joy.

Awakening to the Holy Spirit

Each seeker understands spirituality in differing ways. The goal of spirituality as to respond to the movement of the Holy Spirit within us. The completion of the work of Jesus for our salvation happened at Pentecost when the Spirit became our director. Read Galatians 5:25. As an eight-year-old convert, my notion of serving God was shallow. The Holy Spirit enables for us to recognize Jesus as Lord.

A new sort of awakening begins. The more open minded we are, the more we invite in and benefit from grace. Coincidences are a form of divine communication. We might discover grace in our work. We experience a miracle as something surprises us and delights us. We are seduced by the dreams of what could be and blind to what was the reality. Grace can protect us. It gives us a new perspective. Grace makes us respectful for differing points of view. Being a retired ordained minister, I empathize with their challenges. I know how frustrating and uncomfortable it is to think as though you have not completed your calling. From my own perspective, I understand what we wrestle with in our own lives as training for how we can serve others later. Be open and receptive of restored grace in living now. Restoration is a progressive transformation into Christ. Jesus becomes our brother. Together with Jesus, we are led to the pinnacle of all human achievements which is union with God. The fruit of the Spirit makes this self-giving surrender result. Living a deep spiritual life makes response to God's love possible. Making an informed professor of faith leas to the saving grace of baptism. This is the beginning of being reoriented. The past is corrected. We are forgiven.

As members of God's family, being saved is a personal response to a personal God. To respond to God means to become alive to God. Sin separated us from the unique source of life. Courage is needed for love. Love is an intention and an act of illuminated wisdom. Whatever happens in a long lifetime has been planned from all eternity. Read Galatians 5:16-23. The grace of God in Christ saves us from being helpless before the power of sin. Christians must be watchful of our inner motivations to discern whether experiencing this relationship they flow comes from the Holy Spirit. Read II Corinthians 3:4-6. An unweakened person is acquainted with Jesus, but they are not intimate friends. Seeking souls refer to this as being "born again." The question I often get from seasoned members of churches is "what does 'being born again' mean?"

Restoration of our joy unveils evidence or proof of grace. Everything happens for a reason. Surprising events occur that become evidence of grace in life. Restore your view of your past from your new perspective. Challenges are blessings in disguise.

Restoration means restructure and changing of form. Ultimately it is a shift from living to arrive somewhere to life as an expression of our being. As we transform, awareness and consciousness are restored. We become more empowering, more creative, and more choice. We expose our vulnerability. The dysfunctional realities become easier to deal with. Difficult work is required. We must be real not fake.

Freedom from all-or-none thinking. Clear boundaries. Improved self-esteem. Resolve conflict. Trusting appropriately. Getting needs met. Taking responsibility. Knowing what is appropriate. Restoration is a life changing discipline. It transforms vital areas of our lives. The process is flowing and spontaneous, focused, joyful, assertive, personal, and respect and dignity. As we are restored, we begin to integrate our changes into living in joy. (M. Scott Peck, *The Road Less Traveled: A New Psychology of Love*, pp. 4-8)

Salvation is never static. Being saved is dynamic. It either grows or stagnates. Our response to Christ must be an irrevocable commitment. Christ works in us a work of transformation. We will integrate the fruit of the Spirit making room for God. Integration of Christ causes each of us to be enthusiastic. Kind. Loving. Joyous. Adventurous. We know the life of perfect friendship with Jesus. There comes an increased zeal to serve God in everything we do. We will always know temptation. Jesus experienced temptation. The apostle Paul understood temptations as being unique opportunities to experience the power of Christ. Read II Corinthians 12:710.

The Spirit continues the work of Jesus. God the Father created us. The son Jesus redeemed us. The Holy Spirit restores us to holiness. Read John 16:6-7. How do we recognize the Spirit? The Spirit directs our inner actions. Memory. Feelings. Imagination. Intellect. Will. When we desire and love God even in difficult times, we are responding to the movement of the Spirit.

Integration of Joy

I wrote my Doctor of Psychology dissertation at Christ Church College of the University of Oxford. My title was *Integration of Joy in Clinical Family Counseling*. One day I might turn it into a book. To integrate means to make whole from separate parts. Integration moves us into wholeness. To integrate is the opposite from chaos and confusion, which was ours before our restoration. At the integration stage, we are who we are. We are restored to set limits as is appropriate. It is an ongoing process in the here and now. We awaken numerous times. Regression makes us think we are going backwards. Restoration requires three to five years in my experience as a therapist. (James

E. McReynolds, unpublished dissertation titled *Integration of Joy in Clinical Family Counseling*, 2000)

How are we blocking our own restoration? Is there a problem that needs to change? Who will support your change? We must be open and receptive to the means of grace for our lives. Find clear examples of how we can face this challenge with wisdom, courage, and strength. We can choose to go back to sleep, or to wake up and move on to another dimension of consciousness. (John Faukhauser, *From a Chicken to an Eagle: What Happens When You Change*, p. 46)

When we review relationships that become spiritual restoration agents, we develop a new understanding of how people you met serve an important purpose. God speaks to us through people. We discover evidence of grace in interactions we experience. These people show unyielding love and support. They leave a mark on our souls. In the illuminating light of grace, we know dramatic evidence of how God is directing and protecting us. Every time we acknowledge our brokenness, and we bring it to God for healing restoration, we are given a new opportunity with our sin.

We are influenced by those who stand by us when we find it hard to believe in ourselves. These types of people play a major role in the direction our lives take. Every day we receive feelings, intuitions, nudges, or messages from God in us. Even if we make choices that don't work out, by taking your intuition seriously, we prove we are paying attention. Act before you talk yourself out of something that brings you and other an atmosphere for miracles and joy.

Every day we receive gifts of grace. People are chosen to plant seeds for your spiritual development. Every conversation we have becomes more than an exchange of thoughts and ideas. Conversations become a kind of communion that changes us for the better. Life gets easier. Fear melts away. We feel peace. We no longer possess the notice that we are in control. God steers me in my way to go when I take my hands off the wheel. If we do not learn to surrender our will, we will surrender our peace. To abandon our way for the right way requires a leap of faith. Paying close attention to the inner voice makes way for Divine wisdom.

Learning to surrender does not require a long series of difficult steps. "Help me accept the things I cannot change" will suffice to help us let go. Whenever things do not fall into place, use that time to practice patience. Remind yourself that things happen for a good reason. My departed mom used to say,

"Haste will the place of something better born from grace." When we let go of old things, better things come into our lives.

The issue is clear. We need a restoration to stop acting by reflex, rather than making decisions from an inner-directed, more centered place. Honoring our commitments and walk each other home to grace. Trust that all that has happened exactly as it should. Our prayer is, "I trust you loving God. Please allow this or something better to occur. Amen." Close your eyes. Bring your attention inward.
Give your attention to messages, signs, or little inklings that signal what you need to do. Grace is wrapped in unexpected packages so be willing to dig deeper to uncover your gift.

Restoring balance required discipline. I focused on my need and commitment to relax. I needed to simply be. When I surrendered my need to make things happen. I allowed grace to lead me. Retreat from your busy life long enough to experience the insight that results from having a reserve of physical and emotional space. Moments of blissful joy demonstrated to me that I had merged with love.

The Holy Spirit and a soulmate, who commits to stand by us as we navigate through these brief years on earth, supports us in staying true to the voice of our souls. A soulmate doesn't have to be some romantic partner. The soul-restoring agent shares our values speaks the same language, and we challenge each other to live our best possible lives. Remember that grace-filled restoration often arrives in unexpected places.

God Is Transforming Us

Jesus wants us to encounter him. He desires this encounter his infinite love for us. His invitation to surrender our lives. His call for us to be restored. His loving requirement to repent. His mercy and forgiveness heal us. We are restored to become like him.

Imagine a cold steel bar and a hot burning fire. When we place the cold rod into the hot fire, something happens. The rod becomes like the fire and glows. This fire from the rod can start a fire itself. Imagine the fire as God and we are the steel rod. When we are living in Christ, we begin to take on the character of God. The gifts and fruit of the Spirit begin in our lives. When we touch other, the encounter sets hearts on fire.

Living in joy for the earliest disciples are shared in Acts 2:42. The apostle's teachings, the breaking of bread, fellowship, and prayer. Jesus said, "Apart from me, you can do nothing." John 15:5. Intimacy with God breaths Christ's life into us so that we know it is God's work, not ours.

When we become open to the grace of God, a change happens. The process of restoration can be quite profound. Relationships end. Careers are overhauled. There is an awakening. We seek to know who I am, why am I here, what choices do I have? The road is a rocky one. Stumbling. Falling. Backing up. Spiritually awakening. Writing in a notebook or a journal gives surprising insights. Record patterns of thinking. Record events and people who cause you trouble. Reflect on problems you have been blind to or have been in complete denial. Your soul will receive a miraculous message that you are valuable, and you will gain a perspective of what is working and not working. We open a channel for restoration and divine wisdom as guideposts for life.

Restoration doesn't happen in our heads. It happens in our hearts. We need to deal with uncomfortable feelings. Learning to connect the head and the heart requires perseverance and patience. Rigid walls built around the heart begin to soften. We believe that we can change. (Kay Wilber, *Eye to Eye: The Quest for a New Paradigm*, pp. 125-130)

Books are a conduit for restoration. They can open our hearts and minds to a new way of thinking and being. Books appear at a time when we need them. Only by the grace and power of God do books get into the hands of people who want to live with joy. Everything happens for a reason. Looking back, we see that the resources, events, and people who appear during our soul's restoration journey hold clues for future endeavors.

The year we moved from Bristol, Virginia where I was pastor of the Saint Luke United Methodist Church and began to be the pastor for the First Christian Church in Pawnee City, Nebraska, I used a unique book written by John Killinger. *Raising Your Spiritual Awareness through 365 Simple Gifts from God* reveals that restoring our souls is not as otherworldly as people think. We restore our sensitivity the simple gifts that God gives us. Life is brighter. Dearer. Clearer. Beautiful. Surprising. Simpler. Dr. Killinger, who is now 88 years, writes that old age is the time that we realize the wonder and grace of life. They are being like children again. We compete with others. We attempt to live the best lives for ourselves. We forget how little we really need for living in joy.

Restoring spirituality involves seeing, feeling, tasting without a magical attitude.

We discover the quiet places with Jesus. Spirituality is restored one step at a time. Devotional books do not aim to give us a brand-new life, but to have this life transformed. I once heard John Killinger described as "a knower of many things." Readers are awed by a 328-page book that features gifts such as aprons, donkey, bowing, bubbles, consensus, daydreaming, eyeglasses, feathers, fonts, gargoyles, hair, icebergs, knotholes, masks, naps, neologisms, peacocks, porches, rocks, spiders, swamps, teapots, truckers, watermelons, windmills, and wrinkles.

This wise preacher and teacher wrote, "As you awaken your spiritual sensitivities, you will become more aware of the evidence of God's creative genius in everything your eyes behold." (John Killinger, *Raising Your Spiritual Awareness through 365 Simple Gifts from God*, pp. 5-8).

Uncertainty about the future will be restored with the comfort and security of knowing that we are not alone. We have a higher purpose for living. We can face any challenge. We experience a renewed sensitivity to beauty, deep inner peace, and a feeling of connectedness to all living things.

Most young therapists use popular therapies that feed appetites rather than giving us fresh ways to experience the world. Counseling centers promise far more than they give. People who live in joyless misery who are hurting will spend thousands of dollars. Unhappy people cannot distinguish between genuine restoration and the development of mere coping mechanisms.

Janalea Hoffman, a music therapist, and I taught a course in Guided Imagery and Music for four years at Missouri Western State University in Saint Joseph. Guided imagery is using your imagination, perhaps with selected calming music for use when you are afraid to live and love. Resentful. Overburdened. Criticism. Encouragement. Reasons for doing good. Under pressure. Powerless. Sadness. Past regrets. Rejection. Moodiness. Unanswered prayer. Overlooked. Lack of progress.
Assurance. Unfair labels. Restoration. (S. K. Williams, *The Practice of Personal Transformation*, pp. 120-136)

People find guided imagery has helped when they keep alive hurts and grudges from the past. It helps when they grumble about unpleasant people. They tend to wish that some magic wand would be applied that would change them. They are always worried about the future with anxiety. They report how their useless expenditures of energy are visualized as wasteful as leaving the lights on when nobody's home.

Fragged nerves, frustrations, mismanagements are abated with the use of guided imagery. The memory is soothed, and the mind and soul are free to be attentive to the Holy Spirit in the present to the possibilities of God restoring us. Read I Peter 4, 7. Discouragement is a common source for restoring us to joy. If we continue to give in to it, discouragements bring on spiritual sickness. Anger. Enervation.

Jealousy. Envy. Overeating. Drinking problems. Workaholism. Pouting. Televisionish. Challenges and disappointments came into Jesus' life. "The joy of the Lord," will be our strength. God gave the strength to Jesus and God will give this gift to you. Guided imagery became part of my preaching that added power for listeners and seekers to live with joy and encouragement. One of my members was using a psychotherapist to deal with her discouragement. She told her therapist that she was greatly helped by guided imagery in her pastor's sermons. The therapist said, "Just what kind of church do you go to." She replied, "a church with a spirit of joy."

Permit me to share an example. At the end of a sermon from John 13:21-38, I gave this meditation.

In your imagination, go to a garden inside your neighbor's home. People are enjoying a picnic there. As you enter people are already eating.

You have been invited.

There are twelve people present.

All of them are friends of yours.

One of them is a person you have tried to help.

You feel that you wasted your time.

Let yourself feel the helplessness.

Link your feeling with Christ's sadness over Judas' inaccessibility.

Imagine giving this person the choicest of your food.

Feel the jolt as this person gets up and leaves.

Entrust this person to God. Now realize that someone else, somewhere, sometime, will finally be of help.

Look around to the rest of the company, to the friends and family that you still have.

Keep on keeping on. Don't give up because there is now one less person around the table.

Let Jesus, who is the host, ask for silence.

Jesus gently offers suggestions on how you can continue, even in your discouragement and sadness over a lost friend.

Jesus tells you of opportunities for you to become a humble agent of reconciliation on behalf of others. Let Jesus speak to you now.

(In the space between sentences be silent and listen to healing music or have a musician in the congregation play softly.)

Music is breath to the soul. Christ-seekers learn more theology from the hymns we sang at church during our childhood and youth than any other sources. The Holy Spirit speaks through music. Music sooths the soul. It lifts those who are discouraged. It excites the imagination as it does in guided imagery.

Silence and quiet music induce the soul to experience the presence of God. The imagination is our inner ear that hears better than in the atmosphere filled with sounds. I have found "peace beyond understanding" while sharing joy with Quakers. In worship, they spend time sitting and waiting for the light of the Holy Spirit to send spiritual light. God speaks to the soul in silence. John Killinger is blessed with a poetic soul. Read his poem "Stillness at Connemara."

"Silence rests
Like the gauzy mists
On the bens and the glens And the shining sea.
The air is gathered
To a communion
Of stillness
And I celebrate
Each bird's one call
As it wheels and turns
In the desolate sky
God is thick here
With his presence,
For it is the world And he is not Apart from it.
The bees hymn him
On his throne
And the stone walls
 Hold his kingdom
Together."
(John Killinger, *Raising Your Spiritual Awareness through 365 Simple Gifts from God*, p. 10.

Joy needs community connections to keep it alive. Restoration of joy inspires us to alter the status quo. Norman V. Peale anointed me as the minister of joy to the world. We need to anoint each other with drops of the oil of gladness. This vision of ministry requires a regular, consistent readiness We must address the somberness by gladding others with support, kindness, hope, and encouragement. Read Isaiah 65:17-25.

The gospel of joy offers radical surgery that eludes those who understand only worldly terms. Seekers need clear vision and critical contemplation of what living in God has to offer. This Good News promises no easy answers. It takes time to develop double vision and thinking of things we would rather avoid. Professional therapists do not hold the last word. Complete wholeness and restoration need contemplative commitment. Letting go of some people. Believing that everything comes with a reason. Knowing we are not as free as we think. Detachment. Appreciation. Remembering.

Effective therapists need detachment. The professional licensed counselor insists on it for the sake of objectivity and clarity. Learning to love means to detach. To the world, love is attachment and possession. To bring them and us through the dangers of transference to love just for the sake of love brings healing. Learning to be indifferent to those we attend to is difficult. Shallow therapists offer band-aid cures. In Christ we have no need to lie. So much of so-called spiritual therapy passes on mere information. Restoration and new life are bound to understanding of the other. Those who have problem with food. They refuse to eat but are obsessed with thinking about food. We are not as free as we imagine we are.

Remembering processes growth. The treadmill of repeated acts must be stopped by remembering. We are urged to remember our own past, but to enter a corporate memory that guards our saving stories. The effect of our own journey on earth is our source of woundedness. Often, we are given the joy of a relationship for a brief time. It is short lived, but it happened for a reason. Sometimes the encounter lasts only for seconds. The opportunity for conversion is brief, and life is littered with missed opportunities. Inevitably, we must let go of the things and the people we love most. Everything comes to an end. There is a power stronger than death. In
the presence, we see clearly what love is like. On the front of the bulletin at my beloved brother David's death were the immortal words "love is forever." Facing death gives love a force, a clarity, and an eternal focus.

Prayer becomes an anticipation and participation in our death so that joy is revealed in us. Prayer is the time that eternal joy is revealed in us. Prayer brings intimacy with God. When we understand the life of a believer, we use metaphors such as death and resurrection. In the end, nothing but love matters.

We all are terminal cases. This knowledge lurks in the bottom of our consciousness. We can never cheat death. We may attempt to silence death.

Churches tend to breed infantilism.

Believers are caught in a web between what we have been taught and what our souls tell us. That's what we mean as being "infantile." Seekers are plagued with fear of discontinuity, a sense that things do not hang together. I continue to believe that God has a better road map that any of us do.

What happens when joy needs to be restored? Lamentations 5:15 says, "Joy has gone from our hearts, our dancing is turned to mourning." A joyless state is not a good place to stay over a prolonged period. Joy appears as gone when you just lost a loved one suddenly without warning. Grieving comes because of your tremendous loss. Joy often rises from the ashes of grief. Joy comes at dawn after the dark night of the soul. Your heart laments. Your soul longs for one more conversation. One more embrace. I knew with joy that my brother trusted his life to Jesus. Jesus and joy go hand in hand. Joy comes from obedience and faithfulness to the call of God. Restoration of joy means that we do not grow weary or lose heart. Jesus never forgot the bigger picture of hope for a better tomorrow. Hope ultimately leads to the heavenly joy.

Joy is set before us in the person of Jesus. Stay fixed on Jesus the Christ. Our joy flees when we lose perspective from God. Joy, at the least, lies dormant within every disciple of Christ. When Jesus came into us at our conversion, he brought eternal joy. Now continue to look for an infusion of his eternal joyfulness. Joy is found in God's hopefulness. Pray that joy killers do not rob you of hope. Joy is fully embedded in hope.

Reject the joyless jabs from the revisionists of reality. Seek out the companions of Christ who are set on seeing Jesus as the dispenser of joy. Some circumstances crush joy. Within a community of faith, a Spirit of Joy congregation, we can divert the default toward disillusionment. Seek the reason for your loss. Navigate toward God's lighthouse of love. Joy knows Jesus. We know his love. This is joy. We know his mercy. This is joy. We know his forgiveness. This is joy. We know his faithfulness. This is joy. Joy is knowing our unchanging Christ. When we found Jesus, we discovered joy.

Joy flows from a deeply rooted conviction that not only does God cause all things to work together for good for those who love him. Inherent in joy is te sense of delight in God that can cause us to smile even when things on the outside appear to be falling apart.

God can restore our joy. Joy is found in God's presence. Read Psalm 16:11. When we lack joy, we need to spend time in our chosen place with the spirit of God. Consider God's incredible kindness. Celebrate the power of God. Joy comes out of righteousness. If we have unaddressed sin, it will diminish joy. When we walk with God with a clear and clean conscience, joy is certain. Read Psalm 97:11.

Restoration of joy leads to delighting in the Word of God. Read Psalm 119:11. These biblical insights urge me in the direction of joy.

Have you experienced a time when you were involved in a conversation, and suddenly you realized that God had given you wisdom to speak or write with surprising power? The only explanation is that God is now speaking through you and your gifts. When our words are filled with godly wisdom, they produce joy. Answered prayer brings joy. We cannot receive answered prayer unless we pray. Making time to pray gives us is the method of making room for joy. Prayer unlocks the anticipation that God will do something good. When the Holy Spirit is working in our lives, we produce joy. Read Philippians 1:3-5. When I think of the people God has put into my life, it brings me joy. I thank God for those who have encouraged me, served with me, and developed me.

Placing trust in God brings joy. Read Psalm 40:4. We have a God who loves us more than we can imagine. Our God has promised to help us if we trust his care and wisdom.

Joy is the energy of present redemption and restoration. In Hebrews 12, we are urged to run with perseverance the race set before you. The Hebrews struggled with the temptation to abandon their Christian faith because of the persecution. Read Hebrews 12:1-4. The writer suggested that what gave Jesus the strength to withstand abuse and inner torment was the anticipation of future joy in heaven.

Jesus willingly gave up joy he knew in his relationship with God and with others to receive the joylessness of grief from the events of his crucifixion and death. Jesus knew deep joy in his relationship with his Father. Jesus finally cried out with a climatic cry of dereliction, "My God, my God, why have you forsaken me?" His joy was restored on the far side of the valley of suffering and death, flowing from his renewed intimacy of sitting forever on the right hand of God. Hebrews 2:10 says that many children were brought to glory because of Jesus' work of salvation.

That reflection of glory was flanked by his prior experience of relational joy and the subsequent experience of victorious joy.

The originality of Christian joy

While preaching in Scotland, my mind went back to something I read from an Edinburgh secondhand bookstore. The old book was *The Originality of the Christian Message*. The author was the theologian H.R. Mackintosh. The book was a collection of a series of lectures he gave after World War I on how Christianity is unique, distinctive, or original among the religions of the world. It is not a book that modern scholars or publishers would write or publish.

Mackintosh's volume focuses on what set earliest Christianity apart from other religious movements of first century Rome. Mackintosh proposes that the most distinctive feature of the early Christian movement was its message of redemption as a present experience. The assertion of bodily life beyond the grave makes Christian faith different. Salvation is presently available as spiritual and emotional transformation. He calls this "blessedness," the blessedness of union with God in Christ here and now. The emphasis on joy and rejoicing in the Christian community was highly unusual in the environment of the Greco-Roman world.

Macintosh wrote in accounting for this experience the New Testament authors placed an overriding emphasis on the role for faith. It is by faith that believers are united with Christ in his death and resurrection, find restoration from the guilt and power of sin, and are empowered to "walk in newness of life." Romans 6:4. Faith is quite important. Mackintosh draws attention to something else in the New Testament descriptions of present redemption. I smiled as I read that he emphasized the role of joy.

The Roman world was marked by a sense of darkness, fear, pessimism, and superstition. Bloodshed and extreme cruelty were everywhere. In contrast, the New Testament is "the most obviously exultant book that has been ever written." (H. R. Macintosh, *The Originality of the Christian Message*, p. 116)

He cites Philippians 3:1, 4:4. Paul gives the injunction "to rejoice" three times. This emphasis on joy and rejoicing was unusual in the environment of the time. The fact is so distinctive that scholars have defined the method as "salvation by joy." Macintosh wrote, "The joy I God generated by the fact of Christ was a new phenomenon in religious history, and one changed with boundless significance for the creation of living and victorious morality." *Ibid.*, p. 117.

Reasons for Joy

If we could ask where the early Christian experience of irrepressible joy came from, the answer is to be found in four sources.

The first source of joy was the unshakeable belief the first believers had in the bodily resurrection of Jesus from the dead. They knew in their deepest part of their souls was proved beyond all question. This gave them immense hope for the future. Read I Corinthians 15: 53-56.

The second source of joy was the awareness of having received a radical forgiveness of sins and deliverance from the compulsion of sin. Romans 8:1-4.

The third reason for joy was the experience of belonging to a new social community, the body of Christ, an intriguing kind of society. Read Galatians 3:28 and Colossians 3:11. Membership in this community brought assurance of mutual support and solidarity. Those Christians possessed a newfound dignity and equality that cut across all the deepest social divisions of the day.

The fourth source of early Christian joy was the indwelling and empowering presence of the Holy Spirit. Read Romans 5:5. Perhaps we need to preach on the Holy Spirit which is the source of the fruit of the Spirit.

These are four interconnected realities that generated this contagious joy that distinguished the early Christian movement. They certainly did not have a monopoly on joy. Every person on earth has the capacity to receive the gift of joy, irrespective of religious commitment, because we are all made in the image of God.

At Yale Divinity School's studies on joy, professors kept insisting that joy is not unique to Christians. Still in my long years of studying joy, I know there is a uniqueness to Christian joy experiences. Christian joy is human joy on steroids. The steroidal injection is comprised of the four realities that I just mentioned. Joy is the immersion in the pulsating life and power of the Holy Spirit.

Joy is an experience that coexists with distress and suffering. The New Testament writers repeatedly express that joy and suffering are simultaneous realities. Read II Corinthians 8:1-2 and I Thessalonians 1:6. Joy comes in our times of trials and in te midst of suffering. Sorrow is still sorrow. Pain is real. It hurts. Suffering is accompanied by inextinguishable joy. Read II Corinthians 4. Joy is beyond description and full of glory. Read I Peter 1:18.

Joy was the recurring theme in the teaching and preaching of Jesus. He celebrated with people everywhere their inclusion in the restoring and renewing work. Read Luke 7:31-33, Matthew 11:18-19, Mark 2:15-17.

Seventy of Jesus' followers returning from a preaching and sharing mission "returned with joy, saying, 'Lord, in your name even the demons submit to us!'" Jesus responded by explaining that they have been given access to his own unique authority over spiritual evil, but he told them to not rejoice in their power but rather to "rejoice that your names are written in heaven." Afterward, Jesus addressed God in prayer rejoicing in the Holy Spirit. He marveled how the Father had drawn such marginal and insignificant people into the obit of the saving restoration. These disciple's joy comes from being caught up in "the present blessedness" of God's salvation. Their joy persisted in the face of persecution, social exclusion, and pain. Joy fueled the social radicalism of God's restoration. Discovering the saving activity of God in Jesus elicits great joy. This joy impels a radical change of lifestyle. As ministers of joy to the world, we reinvest our entire lives in the agenda of God's new order in the kingdom of God.

In Jesus's proclamation and instruction on the kingdom, he insisted on an ethical response from his hearers. He called for repentance and faith for our restoration. Read Mark 1:14-15. Repentance entails a conscious refocusing of our values, priorities, allegiances, and patterns of conduct.

Jesus emphasized four areas of human existence. He addressed the area of wealth and possessions, which was economic power. He talked about status, prejudice, and privilege, which was social power. He targeted the issue of violence and our attitude toward enemies, which was the arena of coercive power. He spoke of religious performance, which is the domain of spiritual power.

Responding to the kingdom of God requires major transformations. Jesus' demands were radical. Joy brings discovery. Grace. Gifts. The motivation for commitment to kingdom living is the joy of being connected to Jesus and filled with the Holy Spirit.

Joy is the energy of the kingdom of God.

Joy does not restore by itself. Joy is complemented by discipline, hard work, and courage. Discipleship is difficult. Discipleship comes with a cost. However, we do get joy, the joy of being joined with Jesus and God's people are filled with his holy spirit. This joy sustains us through the darkest hours. Joy is constantly replenished by the love of God "poured into our hearts through the Holy Spirit that has been given to us." Romans 5:5.

Make your living place a haven for joy givers. Retreat from energy suckers. Be energized by positivity. Energy givers are upbeat, optimistic, and this kingdom originated energy will strengthen. Negative emotions steal your energy. Energy is an indication of wellness and wholesomeness. Our whole being, our soul takes in the joy, and we know that we are truly alive. The living energy is the juice, the passion that awakens our cells every morning. Energy flows from your body and soul.

Choose regular exercise to restore yourself. Hugs and loving touches are critical. Your skin is the largest organ in the body. From birth, the body needs touch. Treat your whole self with reverence. The body is the temple that contains your spirit. Without your body, you have no life on earth. If it functions well and remains healthy, then you will have more energy to do your spiritual ministry. Thank your body for keeping you going. Apologize and repent for the stresses you have put it through. Drink pure water. Expose your skin to the sun. Sleep for restoration for the next day.

Each of us must look at Jesus. We must listen to him again and again. We must allow ourselves to be seduced by what we see had hear. Salvation and continuing restoration mean that we believe so much in Jesus that we join forces and become like his clone. Never stop your commitment to continue the work Christ began to make this world so beautiful, delightful, and full of joy.

Discover for yourself what an awesome and spectacular being you are. There is a big difference between doing acts of kindness and being polite or nice. Kindness is our vulnerability. Personal. Commitment. Engagement. Transformational. Lifestyle. Hope. Joy. Gateway to love. Mercy.

"Accepting and having appreciation for difficult experiences
Can help you get through tough times. Trust us! You may be surprised At how well you
can counteract negative feelings."—Denise Foley

Chapter Five

Gratitude and Joy

Gratefulness is the fuel that saves our souls. Joy in the present is different from momentary pleasure. Joy comes from awe, gratitude, purpose, and appreciation. Being thankful invokes the soul. Soul imbues joy. Joy sustains. Gratitude enables us to grow and expand. Gratitude is a twin of joy that brings warmth and laughter into our lives and in the lives of others. May we be among the people who are grateful for living. Gratitude brings a joyful cycle. The more we feel grateful, the more you want to share and give. We will find endless opportunities to give. The Holy Spirit will help us know what to do. Gratitude is the bolt of joy that teaches us what we need to learn. Living in joy is to exist in grateful expectation. Thankfulness is a journey of the soul. Mother Teresa said, "Joy is prayer. Joy is strength. Joy is love. Joy is a net of love by which you can catch souls. She gives most who gives with joy."

Joy is the magic, the miracle that turns the world into a wonderland. It is impossible to feel joyfulness and negativity at the same time. I watched my daughter Linda when she was learning to walk. She would stand and lift her foot.

She often fell. She blamed nobody, not even her shoe. She gets up and tries again. Finally, she walked.

 When the Chicago Cubs won the 2016 World Series, joy could not be contained. Fans had waited 108 years since the Cubs were champions. Joy is essential for living and well-being. Yet, it is the least studied of human emotions.

The disposition to gratitude is conducive to joy. Grateful people see all of life as a gift. They look for good in their lives. Being in joy requires noticing what brings good. They interpret the good in life in benevolent ways. Positive things are good gifts. When a person interprets benefits in a positive fashion, this enhances the joy experience. Gratitude enables us to live in accordance with our true nature. We live well in attunement with the world which results in joy. Life on earth is a school in which we are to learn how to love like God loves. The pandemic us taught us big lessons. We are in control of nothing.

People who are high on the affective trait of joy can rejoice over many things. They find joy even in difficult situations. The disposition for joy enhances how we appraise life and increase the frequency of gratitude. Gratitude and joy have a reciprocal relationship that results in an upward spiral that enhances well-being. Not only does gratitude promote joy, but joy enhances gratitude. Joy has a spiritual nature. Joy is a spiritual emotion in that joy is an enjoyment not associated with physical sensations of pleasure. I have discovered that physical sensations often result in joy. When we enjoy a glass of wine or drink something good, we see the wine as a divine blessing.

Joy is important to a flourishing life, so it will profit anybody to understand joy. (Paul Ellsworth and Carl Smith, "Shades of Joy: Patterns of Appraisal Differentially Pleasant Emotions," *Cognition and Emotion*, 2, pp. 301-311)

Zig Ziglar spoke at Carson-Newman College. He received utmost attention and gratitude. He said, "It makes no difference where you go, there you are. And it makes no difference what you have, there's always more to want. Until you are happy with who you are, you will never be happy because of what you have."

Thank God for events that seem to be unrelated in time. Gratitude deepens and enlarges life. We are thankful for moments of communion that pinpointed our options. Thank God for suffering shared, for joy that outlasts sorrow, for temptations conquered. God above me. God of Love. God within me. God beside me forever.

There is a connection between joy and gratitude. Read Nehemiah 12:27-43. Joy is God-centered. Joy came to the people because of being in the presence of God, gathered in the temple as purified people. Read verse 43 once more. God was the living and active source of joy. Joy comes in remembering God's faithfulness. The wall had been broken down. The city was empty. Indeed, the joy of God's people comes with thankfulness.

There is more to being grateful than sating thanks for the gifts from God. The attitude of gratitude reveals blessings that we otherwise overlook. Gratitude transforms the methods of how we come to understand living. Joyful people focus on the blessings of their life situations. They experience the circumstances as a transformation. They saw the beauty of ordinariness in their lives. Dwell on an ocean of positive, not a puddle of negatives.

Before we attend school and learn to count with numbers, we are taught to be grateful and to say thanks. Gratitude becomes our way of life. Gratitude begins with training in manners, the learned response to receiving anything. Our minds and souls create deeper capacities. Children show contentment as they receive a birthday or Christmas present. What a wonderful joy to live with a family that expresses joy on love days I which there is no other reason but that they have thankfulness built in. Children enjoy most any gift. My daughter always said, "thank you," even if given sometimes as simple as a pretty rock or a birthday card.

Flourishing as Human Beings

No matter where we find ourselves, we all desire to flourish. The Bible directs our attention to gratitude. Thankfulness is mentioned 150 times. Read I Thessalonians 5:16-18. God directs people thankful. Gratitude emerges as a natural response when we learn of God's grace. The Hebrew Bible reminds us to express gratitude. Read I Chronicles 16:34, Psalm 106:1, Psalm 118:1, 29, Psalm 136:1. God calls loudly and clearly to be thankful. Thanksgiving helps us see good things each day. Thanking savors good things. Gratitude makes us speak often of good things.

Grateful people experience more joy. Being grateful has social benefits, such as stronger relationships. They are more generous and collaborative. More content. More inner peace. Grateful people have more energy. Sleep better. Less health complaints. More alert. Calmer. Increase longevity.

Write down three good things to enhance your well-being. Bless others by expressing gratitude orally or in writing. When was the last time you said thank you? I know I have done it a dozen times today. The more gratitude we feel, the more joy we will experience. Cultivate your own gratitude muscle and learn to focus on what you are thankful for.

The present time is the time to create an opening for feeling gratitude. Allow your thanksgiving to flow. Others will feel your gratitude just by seeing your joyful transformation. Living in gratitude is to touch heaven. In thinking only of ourselves, we expect the world or others to provide what we need. Gratitude will gently cause us to be aware of others and their needs. Gratitude is the opposite of selfishness. It is knowing the grace of God and sharing grace with those around you.

Blessings result from using our spiritual gifts for overcoming challenges, burdens, and difficulties. If we receive our inspiration from God and exercise our gifts, God blesses us, and we bless others. Being grateful is your direct pathway to joy. Imagine that. Everything happens for a reason. Our current life partners and those from our past, our siblings, our friends, our teachers, and our mentors were sent to us as gifts including our vision quest. Bless every relationship and be grateful for them.

God is above the confines of time and space. The more I express thanks the more I am aware of blessings, especially the back door miraculous ones. Deaths that wake up my appreciation of life. Friends who have stood by me. Slow recoveries kept me trusting. The memory of the fragrance of the valentine roses after they died. The challenges that affirmed my beliefs. Parents and loyal friends that never stopped praying for me. Business reversals that have led me to deeper giving. The remarks of fellow clergy that changed my thinking.

Be grateful for God giving us free will. We can choose free will and make any needed changes. Free will comes with responsibility. Use your intuition. Do whatever your insights reveal. If you concentrate on discovering the good in life situations, your life will be filled with gratitude. Every one of the seven billion people populating earth today had the capacity for joy when they were born. See the joy expressed in a baby's face. Joy flows in our faces throughout our lifespans. Joy is contagious.

We turn to catch a leaf, whose pattern is so individual and complex. Thank God for the sunrise nudging dawn away. Red roses. Symphonies of music from the birds. Enthusiasm of scampering squirrels. Rainbows of promise. Our lives would be impoverished without creation. The blessings of the good earth merge with the gospel of joy into the grace of gratitude.

Make a list of things others would make somebody be grateful to you. Find at least five opportunities a day for one week, to say thank you and to really mean it. Write a gratitude letter to someone from your past who impacted your life. Find a gratitude quote and place it where you will see it. Start a gratitude journal. Record the things you are grateful for.

Express gratitude even in these pandemic and challenging times. Be grateful to the physicians and nurses who risk their own lives to save lives locally and globally.

The mystic Meister Eck said, "If the only prayer you say in your life is 'thank you,' that would suffice." Gratitude is thankfulness, counting blessing, noticing simple pleasures, and acknowledging everything you receive. It means learning to live your life as if everything is a miracle. Gratitude is being aware on a continuous basis of how much you have been given. Resist the negative so you dwell only on beautiful things.

Gratitude shifts our focus from what our life lacks to the abundance that is already present. Gratitude causes people to be happier with more joy than can be contained. Each has the possibility of finding treasures where they never searched. They gain wisdom from tongues they were not willing to listen to. Beauty waits to be found where they do not look. We must endeavor to be open to see opportunities. Gratitude is such a powerful experience. It changes attitudes. It brightens outlooks. (Amanda Gore, *The Gospel of Joy*, pp. 14-28.

Nobody lives a perfect life. Acknowledge your thanksgiving in all things great and small. Simply taking time to notice and reflect on the things in your life can change your life for the better. By an expression of gratitude, you will change your perspective by focusing on things that give joy for you. Levels of determination. Enthusiasm. Alertness. Optimism. Energy. Less stress. Grateful people are more creative. They bounce back quickly from adversity. The have a stronger immune system.

To say we are grateful is not to declare that everything in our lives is necessarily at our highest. Gratitude is the best indication that we are fully aware of the many blessings.

We will then notice and appreciate each day's gifts. Most human beings take for granted the goodness that is already present in their lives. Gratitude and joy are like two peas in a pod.

Being grateful does not mean that perfection, but whoever you are, you can accept it as a gift. Everybody enjoys being appreciated. The simplest action of gratitude will change somebody's day. The ministry of bringing joy to the world causes the ungrateful to become grateful. This joy will bring tears from your eyes. Express gratitude for the magnificence of small things.

Stop counting your losses. Start counting blessings. Blessings outnumber your losses for blessings are immeasurable. We experience the mental sunshine of gratitude in others. As we do, we glow with sunshine within ourselves.

When I served as a pastor in Saint Joseph, Missouri, I was assistant superintendent of the Buchanan County Children's Home. The home served children and youth with criminal records, who had little discipline. Most had low self-esteem and they refused to go to school. Discipline was difficult. Rules were tight. Meals were simple. The residents remained angry and in conflict. Most requests were ignored. They had to stay inside the home if they could not cope or started a fight. Some whose crime was just not attending school. Those could ride a school bus to their home after the school classes ended. Most had little or no encouragement from parents. Days were filled with hard work and tension. Nobody expressed appreciation.

One of the things that really helped them was when I'd write, "Thank you for your efforts to cope in a difficult place and situation." Most had never been thanked before.

Chapter Six

Kindness and Joy

Bruce Reyes-Chow, Presbyterian pastor, and author of *In Defense of Kindness*, was our leader at the 2022 Clergy Retreat at Saint Benedict Conference Center in Nebraska. He quoted Ella Wheeler Wilcox, "So many gods, so many creeds, so many paths that wind and wind, while just the art of being kind is all the sad world needs."

We are customed to think of kindness as "being nice" or being polite or sweet. Some people think kindness is that "extra something" that good people weave into their daily lives. Kindness is being who we really are. Kindness can utterly transform our lives and the lives of others through simple acts.

Kind words can be short. They are easy to speak, but their echoes are endless. Children who are taught to be kind. Forever, they will be able to see a stranger as someone special. I am so grateful for children. They are apostles of joy and kindness sent forth to preach of love, joy, and kindness. Read Psalm 127:3. The highest pinnacle of the spiritual life is not just being kind or having joy in unbroken sunshine, but trust that God is always loving us.

Pablo Casals pinned the power of kindness. He wrote, "Each person has inside a decency and goodness. If they listen to it and act on it, they are giving a great deal of what the world needs most. It is not complicated, but it takes courage for a person to listen to their own goodness and act on it."

The Power of Random Acts of Kindness

Conari Press, a California publisher, offered a book, Random Acts of Kindness, written by scores of little-known writers. they chose the ones that offered the widest reflections on kindness. The editors choose each story simply by instinct.

The foundation of each story was a simple and compassionate connection between strangers or were regarded as family. Each story that I read brought some tears and deep wells of joy.

Bruce helped us realize how kindness spreads from person to person with the potential to light up the whole world. The way we treat others matters. Joy is wrapped in kindness. It makes an eternal mark as someone loved us unconditionally, as the spark of kindness passes on and on. (Bruce Reyes-Chow, *In Defense of Kindness*, pp. 1-15)

Part of what holds people back from being kind is how unattractive the concept sounds. Being proud of being kind sounds like something we settle on only when every other, more robust ambition has been exhausted. This very wrong suspicion has been around for a long time. Kindness for some indicates one who has failed. (Alain de Botton, *The School of Life: An Emotional Education*, p. 99)

Loving Kindness Takes Time

Kindness is best done in the easiest way possible. The experience springs forth naturally and gently. Sometimes kindness feels glorious. Most of the time it is ordinary. Expand your awareness to every child of God on earth. Some we may like. Some we won't like. Mark Twain said, "Kindness is the language which the deaf can hear and the blind can see."

Kindness brings on gratitude. A pastor who attended a silent retreat in a Missouri monastery observed that the cost of the meal was not included. The presenters came to share with their family of six. He volunteered to pay for the lunch for everyone including the participants. He said, "I noticed the joy it brought me to consider giving such a gift."

Kindness has a ripple effect. Every person has opportunities to be kind to others. We find it a God-based mystery to know how kindness affects others. Those ripple effects of kindness affect the people we encounter, and those that they encounter after they leave us. Read Luke 7:36-50. Kindness helps us entering relationships that are short time or long time. We encourage the wholeness of anybody whom we encounter anywhere for any purpose, at any time, no matter what the situation is.

Be willing to walk away from any situation. Walking each other home and stepping out of our routine with a kind action. Kindness deepens our connection to everyone. Christ never missed a chance to show kindness. The epiphany of your kindness was as you answered your mother's request to show kindness to the wedding guests.

Choosing to be kind in this world is not easy. It takes your energy away. Sometimes being kind is impossible. When human dignity is restored, kindness will be embraced. Examine the complexities of unkind persons before you decide to judge them. Kindness requires us to observe what is needed. One chapter in Christie Watson's book is "Everything you can imagine is real." (Christie Watson, *The Language of Kindness*, pp. 42-74)

A wealthy man called Simon the Pharisee invited a host of guests for fellowship and dinner. Jesus was there. A woman began weeping and her tears fell on the feet of Jesus. She was simply overcome with emotion. She loosened her long hair and started to wipe the tears with her hair. This act was sensation and would not be acceptable behavior. Women of the time let down their hair as an indication that anything, including a sexual encounter, was unconditionally offered.

We shall never find a person filled with joy, who is unkind. Kindness is the one component of joy that has no substitute. Kindness is our set point if we are to know the bliss of joy. Life depends on the kindness of others. The source for courageous living is found in the kindness of others. The smallest kind expression makes the biggest difference.

Kindness is defined as an intentional and selfless kind of gentle loving joy that involves concentrating on the needs of another. You should be kind to people on your way up because these are the same people you will be seeing again on your way down.

Joy can be ignited again, suddenly, surprisingly by a simple caring touch of another person. We see God in everything that surrounds us. We see love given and received. Kindness is no small achievement. It is indeed a lifelong effort. Be assured that God is always seeking us. In every aspect of life, we communicate by what we, not want we say. I often hear people say, "Be aware of body-language. The body does not lie. Every bodily gesture, expression, motion, quirk, even our breathing communicates what we are feeling. Read Mathew 25. How many of us see the face of Jesus in hungry people or imprisoned people? Such faces are like all human faces is the face of Christ.

When we profess faith, our profession is bound up with how we treat each other. We must discover by ourselves how to feed the hungry, to give drinks to the thirsty, forgive our enemies, and to do goodness and kindness to those who persecute us. The Holy Spirit teaches us what means for us to love, to be just, and to be a peacemaker. Paradoxically, the soul is fed not by consuming but by giving. Joy is not something to hold only for ourselves. Joy is a life-giving energy. The more it is shared, the more is generated. As your minister of joy, I view kindness is not a fruit of the Spirit to be kept, but a living way of life to be expressed in all our relationships for a long, long time, the rest of our lives.

Jesus provided an example of kindness by coming to earth. Jesus gave us the chance to experience ultimate joy. Kindness helps us experience who God made us to be. Kindness requires us to be less ourselves. Read Romans 5:1-5.
Be kind to yourself. Ann Lamott said, "Almost everything will work again if you unplug it for a few minutes, including you."

Joy is a journey. Marianne Williams wrote, "Joy is what happens to us when we allow ourselves to recognize how good things really are." Joy is an exuberant and focused expression of happiness. Acts of kindness warm our hearts, bring smiles to faces, and remain on the videos of our souls.

Kindness is a lifestyle. A daily practice. A choice. A faithfulness. A habit of goodwill. Intentionality. Unplanned. In the moment. Kindness requires a seeking out, looking out for the needs of others. The collection of stories of kindness began in California in 1982. Anne Herbert scrawled the words, "practice random kindness and senseless acts of beauty," on a napkin in a restaurant.

The kindness of God in Hebrew scriptures is loyalty and love that expands generations to draw us back to God. Kindness is steadfast love that endures. Kindness equals patience. Kindness redeems and restores. There is no doubt that random acts of kindness make the world a better place to live. The "joy of the Lord" comes with more than random acts of kindness. The steadfast kindness of God is the determination to be present in the world to restore and redeem.

Kindness is related to the word "kind." Also, the word "kindred." Kindness is love, loyalty, for people "of your own kind." We are children of God, and we are connected to all creation and all people. Jesus caused kindness to be global. Read John 3:16. According to Jesus, joy is to go from Jerusalem, Judea, Samaria, and to the ends of the earth.

It is the prayer of this writer that these words are tugging at the sleeve of your mind about ways you can intentionally show kindness. Joy is the emotion that depends on what happens inside us. We know an appreciation for the little things in life. We are connected to God and one another. We feel a sense of belonging, connecting, and joying within. Amelia Earhart said, "A single act of kindness throws out roots in all directions, and the roots spring up and make new trees."

We all have an impact on the world around us. Living with kindness is the intention of my life. Bringing joy to the world connects me with others who are on a similar path. Kindness is a powerful force that transforms the world. Every act of kindness is like a stone falling in a lake. Ripples go out far beyond what we can see, but we know that they will affect everything.

Peter W. Marty wrote as he was watching a documentary on kindness shown in Geel, Belgium. "For over 700 years, the small city has been welcoming people with mental illness, many of whom arrive with severe mental disorders. Most of the townspeople don't look at these individuals as psychiatric patients so much as family members. The call them boarders or guests. Families take them into their homes in something akin to a foster care program for adults. 'To us, this is normal,' said Christel Syen, a store owner. 'We all grew up with boarders. We don't know any other way.'

"A 14th century church in Geel is dedicated to Dymphna, the patron saint of te mentally afflicted. According to legend, this seventh-century Irish princess, who fled to Geel to escape her incestuous father, used her considerable resources to build a hospital for the poor and sick. Versions of the legend suggest she offered personal care for mentally tormented individuals who were shunned by medieval society.

"For centuries, scholars have been fascinated by the hospitable attitude of the Geel citizenry toward those with chronic mental illness. Mental differences are routinely accepted. Behaviors stigmatized and feared elsewhere are normalized. It is the ultimate community-based model for mental health. A psychiatric hospital in town provides higher-level care for those who are violent or those experiencing a crisis Today, nearly 300 boarders live with more than 200 families." (Peter W. Marty, "Saint Dymphna's Care," *The Christian Century*, January 12, 2022, p. 3)

Christie Watson, nurse, wrote about the true meaning of a nurse's life. Her book, *The Language of Kindness: A Nurse's Story*, she shows the joys and the difficulties of looking after people at their most vulnerable times. Read Luke 6:36.

Kindness includes the long struggle to grow in compassion. From the beginning of time, God's creations were to be reflections of God. Being created in God's image, we have the responsibility toward ourselves and others. The sadness linked with kindness and compassion occurs when this image is forgotten or lost. What if we looked at others with the eyes of God? Read I John 4:8. Love is without qualification. Every human is created by love, for love, and in love.

If we have lived our lives with love surrounding us, we are blessed. If we are not so blessed, it is difficult to paint an accurate picture of the love of God. It is a puzzle to understand love for those who reject salvation.

Image and love are inseparable. Our compassion is deeply rooted in the conviction that all humans are meant to receive the fruit of the Spirit. Love ignites our kindness and compassion. Without love, the image of God is lost, and we are not able to see it. Love is God. God does not change the truth in the face of being sinned against, unknown, despised, and rejected. We are given free will to darken the image, hide it. Forget it. Being kind and compassionate never asked us to ignore sin. It demands a recognition of God's image in those we love. We are tempted to despise, keep at a distance, and ignore. Just one drop of compassion for those who sin, those who miss the mark, and those who are ignorant, demands more than human efforts could ever achieve.

That is why God sent Jesus. The gospel of joy can be puzzling. Jesus was deeply aware of sin. He knew where sinners would eventually cause him death on a cross. His compassion saw far into the future. The compassion Jesus demonstrated was for the physically ill, the mentally ill, and the spiritually ill. Read Mark 6:34.

Doing acts of kindness will not guarantee that we'll receive kindness in return. If we are kind so that we receive and expect repayment, we will know a lifetime of frustration. Kindness is a fruit of the Spirit. It is rarely reciprocated in our culture.

Kind people are my kind of people. One of the ministers who attended the clergy retreat for 2022 gave our regional minister, Christopher Morton, a poster containing these words. Kind people touch the lives of others: teachers who open minds to truth. Writers who depict life as it is. Doctors who aid the healing process. Ministers who break the bread of life. Artists who show us as we are. Therapists who bring together our separate selves.

Kind people enrich our lives. The gift of kindness, a fruit of the Spirit, is given to all. What I regret most in my life are failures of kindness. Those moments when another person was there, right in front of me, suffering or feeling shame, and I responded with little strength and courage. Be kind. Make your little mark on this huge world just by being you.

A good deed is never lost. One who sows courtesy reaps friendship. One who plants kindness gathers love. Sometimes the good that one does, comes back in the form of a surprising miracle.

Chapter Seven

Delight and Joy

Sometimes we overlook the delights of joy during our busy lives. Write in your journal about the joys of moments of delight. What is this joy? Joy is those delightful moments when our alienation from people goes away. This is a "joyning." When we experience delight, we desire to share it. What is giving you delight today? Sharing will shift your day to one of joy. Joy is emotional delight. Feelings of gladness. Felicity. Unanticipated good.

Delight is joy. The roofs resound with delight. Cool expressions of joy include bundle of joy, joygasm, cocky's joy, joystick, jumping for joy, overjoy, joyance, to feel joy, and to rejoice. Joy is the emotion of great delight caused by something good. Joy is the delightful and infallible sign of the presence of God.

The more we study delight, the more delight there is to study. Jesus and his church offer a special way of being. Delight is self-validated, needing other justification but the experience described is joy as delight. (B. I. Frederickson, "What Good Are Positive Emotions?" *Review of General Psychology*, 2, 1998, pp. 300-319)

The six congregations in my Max Meadows Circuit in Virginia wanted to have more frequent communion. Some of the church board members said they did not find having communion often was a helpful idea. I asked if that same logic included times for eating and drinking. Communion offers food for the spiritual self. Is that true of lovemaking with your spouse? For me to ask that direct question is confessing that a couple has never been in love. That was my way of our sharing love and delight.

The process of sanctification brings a falling in love with God. Sexual delight intensifies the desire for a joyous union of a different kind. Salvation involves discipline. "Being saved" starts with a lostness, an emptiness, a lack and desire for something eternal and better. This world cannot heal our aches and soul yearnings.

The world teases us with false promises. That causes us to be even less satisfied and without the contentment for a joy that needs no justification other than the experience of joy. Our restlessness intensifies our search for

God with the spiritual lure of joy. Joy is the flame of divine love. The joy of the Lord fulfills its promise with anticipation which nothing finite can fulfill. God's promise is a life of everlasting joy.

Joy dances. The language of spirituality is a way of putting into words things we do not understand. We delight in forcibly suppression our own beliefs.

We cultivate joy by abiding in Christ. Joy is a delightful fruit of the Spirit. Joy is a life choice. It is rooted in the delight of the goodness of God. The more ways that we develop a personal relationship with God, the more joyful living will result. We find joy by resting in the providence of God. We cultivate joy by realizing that our ways are not God's way. The ways of God are higher than ours. God's understanding is greater than our understanding. God will accomplish God's good plans and purpose for our lives. Scripture tells us that "all the trees of the field will clap their hands."

Everything is jumping with unbridled joy. Delight shines as our hearts and souls beat to the same song of joy. Jesus certainly experienced joy. Jesus shared in the delight of the blind receiving their sight. Lame ones were dancing in delight. Jesus came to reclaim the joy that sin had stolen.

We delight in joy in the present by remembering that there is a future reality waiting for us where there is a new heaven and a new earth created, where we eventually enter the joy of God's unveiled eternal presence. We bask in that joy now, even as we look forward to its fullness in the courts of heaven.

Joy as delight is impossible unless one goes through the process with a profound thirst. The joy of each disciple grows in proportion to the joy of all people. Joy itself is at the heart of faithful evangelism. Joy is participation in the kingdom of God. The process of salvation is a life-long purification.

Joy is such a precious emotion that a person with delight will glow. So, it is with the Spirit of Joy Church. Read Romans 8:38-39. When a church is filled with joy, evangelism is natural, not just a gross salesmanship. We gain with holy intuition that communion with God satisfies the deepest delight. Glorifying God is an eternal enjoyment.

Every believer must do the work as ministers of joy to the world. Someone. Somehow. Somewhere. We shall grow old loving God in divine joy. Joy is delightful divinity dancing in our souls.

Words of Delight

The joy of dancing, singing, and creating a few crazy words or songs to lift us.
Do you have a word of delight that makes you silly-happy? Enjoy. Jubilant. Jouissance. Euphoric. Words and the languages that are made up of words have been created by writers for thousands of years.

There are currently 7,939 languages in the world. Among the seven billion people, three billion of them can read and speak English. Writers are gifted with creating words. Remember "supercalifragilisticexpialidocious" in the Mary Poppins film. *Mary Poppins* is a series of children's books published by an Australian author in 1934. P.L. Travers, the author, wrote to reframe her childhood that was the opposite of a delight. Her mother attempted suicide. Her dad died from a seizure. Walt Disney created the iconic story of a magical nanny who created rhymes and words, pull hat racks from her bag, and carry viewers to delightful adventures.

When living itself holds out illnesses, it affects our coping skills. It steals energy. We need some heavenly delight to get us on our feet again. This eternal delight lifts our gazing eyes away from pitfalls that stall us as we turn our eyes upon Jesus. This joyful delight gives us a fresh resolve, an impetus, and strength enough to keep on.

God delights in our service. God does not need them, but people around us do. Serving others delights as a blessing. Fame, money, and rewards rarely result from humble service. Read Ephesians 2:10. Loving the unlovable is a challenge. We have been bruised and broken. Others have disgraced us. Some have ruined us by the deliberate and thoughtless words and actions. Difficult as it is, we put our feelings aside and pray for others. Delightfully healed by grace, we ask God to forgive them, bless them, and ever prosper them.

Read Psalm 51:8. Sorrow and joy are involved in the doings of God. Read Psalm 126:5. God's delightful promise is that God will turn our sorrow into joy. Joy links heaven and earth, for both can be joyous over the repentance of each sinner. Joy was the rationale for the ministry of Paul. Read II Corinthians 1:24, 2:3, Romans 14:7 and 15:13 to see why Paul made such an impact on the world. The writer of John agrees with Jesus and with Paul that the ministry of joy has no other purpose but that our joy may be full. I John 1:4.

Joy is the defining mark of the church. Joyfulness marks the life of the Christian community. As Christians work together, they are filled with the Holy Spirit. Joy comes from participating in God's ministry in the world. We delight from seeing lives being positively changed and relationships enhanced. Joy marks the people of God both individually and corporately. Joining with God in ministry brings hope and peace and love and joy.

As strange and puzzling living in joy appears, we dare not dismiss it as peculiar to the early church. Jesus modeled the strangeness. Read Hebrews 12:2. Morning joy comes with those who mourn in the night. This is the delightful mystery of the incarnation.

Joy arrives when delightful divinity dances in us. Delight is that sweet moment of being in-between dreams before you awaken. Delight yearns for a better future. Just to breathe is delight. Delight is a winter blue sky with its ember-like glow of the unseen setting sun. I do appreciate little moments when I think of the gratefulness of delight.

Delight is the quiet, quirky calm of newness. I get this whenever I can travel, especially when I share my delights and joys. I even talk to strangers. We might have nothing in common but that we will arrive in the same place. We are united by one path and one moment of living. Finding joy in our sorrows comes from sharing them with one another. The act of sharing stimulates delight. Every day becomes a new beginning. We will discover heaping measures of kindness coming back at us. Delightful reciprocity is experienced everywhere. Read Luke 6:37-38.

"The intimacy of bodies begins with the intimacy of the soul, long conversations, honest stories, common jokes, the right joy, a strong shoulder, a kind word, a delicious tea." -- Pamela Hoffman

Chapter Eight

Human Bodies and Joy

Grace over time has deepened intimacy with my body. Harvard Medical School publishes articles on the joy-health connection. Joy has to do with feeling better and improving health. Harvard researchers see evidence that positive emotion helps us live heathier and longer. Money and material things. Youthfully attractive. Being well known. Having political power. None of these things matter. (Peterson, Christopher and Martin Seligman, *Harvard Health Publishing*, pp. 1-7)

On an emotional level, we feel joy in ways that are tearful, euphoric, contenting, surprising, and unique. Scientifically, we feel joy in our neurotransmitters, tiny chemical cells that transmit signals between or nerves and other body cells. These cells are responsible for processing and feeling in every aspect of the body from blood to digestion. (R. A. Martin, "Is Laughter the Best Medicine? Humor, Laughter, and Physical Health, *Current Directions in Psychological Science*, 11, 2002, pp. 216-220)

These positive benefits include a healthier lifestyle. Boost in the immune system. Eliminating stress and body pain. Longevity. Joy is affected by the brain. Differing emotions involve different brain structures. The body's control panel or frontal lobe monitors our emotional state. The information center that regulates consciousness or the thalamus regulates emotional responses.

Human bodies feel joy because of the release of serotonin and dopamine. When we are in a joy, our face flushes, and the heart races. Butterflies in the stomach, changes in finger temperature, facial expressions depend on our emotions. The effects of the circulatory system can be present in differing ways. The circulatory system consists of blood, blood vessels, veins, heart, and lymph.

The autonomic nervous system is responsible for all the things our body does without conscious effort from us. Dilation of the pupil. Breathing. Digestion. Sweating. Temperature. Salivation. Metabolism. The pupils in our eyes dilate if we are aroused sexually. (J. S. House and Kenneth R. Landis, "Social Relationships and Health," *Science*, 241, 1988, pp. 540-545.

When joy happens, the physical and emotional response occurs immediately, because the joy is happening simultaneously in the body. The urge to jump for joy or to cry with joy. The winning quarterback on the University of Georgia football team could not stop crying as the Bulldogs beat the University of Alabama Crimson Tide for the national division one championship.

Joy and Deep Delight

The gift of joy is a paradox. In the Greek New Testament joy literally means "for the heart, in its deepest place of passion and feelings, to be well." Joy brings a deep sense of delight. However, when a person is "in a joy," it is likely there will be tears. These are the tears of gratitude, satisfaction, and wonder that come from a deep place in the soul. I cried when I found that people all around the world were reading my books on joy. This was so amazing, almost too overwhelming to behold. The body bursts with a release of ecstasy streaming down the face.

Tears of joy cannot be choreographed. Tears simply happen. The body also knows tears of sorrow. Tears of pain. Tears of loss. These human tears burning the eyes like the salt of the sea. The place from which the tears come is as deep as the oceans. Tears expose the deepest longings, losses, and vulnerabilities. Joy is surely a paradox. It brings tears from the same response as sorrow.

Whenever I observe a person crying out of joy or weeping from grief, I join in. We identify with them, and we receive joy ourselves. Our compassion is ignited in memories of our own times of grief. In a joy, tears simply flow.

Human beings need not be taught to cry. Crying is how most of us began life. Tears flow in every age of our living. Tears transcend. Tears come to everyone. All economic backgrounds. Every race. Every class. Any politics. Quality of education. For any age, stature, or family teachings, we learn and relearn to cry. The scriptures tell us that "Jesus wept," when his friend Lazarus died. Jesus' tears fall spontaneously. They flow like a river.

With all the unending wars, pandemics, senseless killings, endless abortions, family anger, and executions, fires, mudslides, automobile accidents, or starvation of a homeless person or one who lives in a third world nation are never brought back to life. The last book of Holy Scripture assures us "there

89

will be no more tears. God will wipe away every tear." In the early church, they called these moments "the gift of tears." Tears are a part of the body's life. Tears may be our most effective prayers. Let the tears come. Crying is a natural response.

Withholding tears is dangerous to health. "Have a good cry" and find joy and positivity Having a good cry releases tension. Tears are evidence not of self-pity, rage, or frustration, but they appear as a gift, and their fruit is always joy.

Tears flow when the creator of life is uncovered when all masks are dropped. We admit our human weakness. Grace enters our experience where we have been wounded. Believers come to the end of their rope. Tears are cleansing. We now see with a clear eye. We receive more than clarity. Clarity of vision and freedom of action. Tears begin to flow when we discover contradiction between what we hope for and what we are. Tears result from waiting for a deep sense of joy. I am given the grace of God for loving myself with the love of God.

Tears find us.

We do not have to look for tears. Tears find us in the best of times or the worst of times. Tears give the body pause. Presence. Aliveness. Jesus weeps for all the children of God. Jesus weeps with us. God is with us in our gift of tears. Tears come from a deep well. Permit the tears when they come. Tears flow into joy. That is a paradox. Joy floods our souls. Joy splashes upon our countenance. Remember your experiences of joy in the past as a gateway to enjoying the present moments of joy. Allow the joy into your soul. Joy opens the doors for more joy.

Joy is a mysterious surprise. It is a wonderful fruit of the Holy Spirit. The heights of our moments of joy will mirror the depth of our sufferings. Uncover the joy. Every single joyful experience is remembered. Each joy reminds of the way that each of us grows, even in these days of high anxiety, rumors of wars, the latest pandemic, and in the last days of our existence.

In a joy, our bodies flood with chemicals that raise our heart rate and blood pressure, keep bodies alert and focused. Chronic stress on the body that leads to exhaustion and illness. Moments of joy give our bodies a break from stress, enabling us to recover. Stress narrows our focus. We ruminate on our worries and fixate on life's challenges. We fail to notice joy.

Our body's emotional response can cause the feelings of anxiousness or despair. We withdraw from emotional support and things we enjoy, which cause us to be even sadder, more anxious, with constant negative feedback. Joy jumpstarts the opposite, positive feedback that leads to connection and well-being. (B.R. Levy and S.R. Kunkel, "Longevity Increased by Positive Self-Perceptions of Aging," *Journal of Personality and Social Psychology*, pp. 261-270)

Our bodies are wonderful monitors of our emotional health. The body never lies.

Emotions, including joy, gets stored in our bodies. We stuff our feelings inside. Those stuffed feelings take up space until we are ready to express them. The process is detrimental to our emotion well-being and our physical health.

Some appear to prefer sickness to wholeness. We become promiscuous and we missed love and think it is too late for change. The poor and hungry see no way out. The aged and senile feel useless and unwanted. Schizophrenics cannot get their parts together. Able-bodied jobless refuse to seek work. The nervous and apprehension will not control their tension. We become prisons in cells we constructed ourselves and refuse to use their keys.

Take a moment to center yourself. Relax your body fully. Turn off the chatter in your brain. Place your hand on your stomach and repeat several times, "Please reveal to me my present emotions." Quietly listen for an answer. Repeat it as much as you feel the need. Drop deeper into your body. Feel warm and relax. Repeat as you feel tight knots as emotions come up. Remember the body does not lie.

If too much emotional energy builds up inside the body, releasing them will present disease or discomfort. Few people want to face the experience of bodily vulnerability. Grace over time deepens intimacy with the body. A slow intentional life is a radical act of witness to another way of existing.

One day the body will die. At 80 years of age, it could be tomorrow, in six months, or in six years. Each day in our quiet times we remember how to cherish life. My body enables us to remember that life is a gift. Take nothing for granted. Feeling accompanying wellness will not last forever. Some of the physical pain will stop. Some of it will continue until when we die.

The Russian writer Fyodor Dostoevsky gives us a vision quest of the experience of joy. The words he wrote in *The Brothers Karamazov* were attributed to a dying Russian Orthodox Church monk.

"My life is ending, but every day that is left me, I feel in touch with a new infinite, unknown, but approaching life, the nearness of which sets my heart quivering with rapture, my mind glowing, and my heart weeping with joy. Kiss the earth and love it. Love it with an unceasing, consuming love. Love everyone. Love everything. Water the earth with the tears of your joy. And love those tears. Do not become ashamed of that ecstasy. Prize it. For it is a gift of God and a great one." Accomplishing impossible feats in my ministry of joy to the world, I work beyond my body's capacity. My body lets me feel the impact. In my remaining days, I keep discovering new layers of how my primary vocation and calling must relish with this old vessel of flesh, bone, and blood.

Life is not about overcoming our bodily vulnerabilities. It is about experiencing the holy in our bodies. Everybody has a fluency in joy. Joy is the pure and simple delight in being alive. Feeling joy in our bodies is living love. (S. T. Lyubomirsky, "The Meaning and Expression of Joy: Comparing the United States and Russia," *American Psychologist*, 56, pp. 239-240)

If you sense lack of love for yourself, feeling unworthy, or bodily pain, scan your body and locate where there is a sensation that needs attention. Emotional discomfort is experienced somewhere in your body. Bodies reveal your need with contraction in your gut, pressure in your chest, or tightness in the throat.

Place your hand on the part of the body where the abnormality is located. Take a few deep breaths. Tap on that place with your fingers. If I do this before I sleep, the sensation decreases. The message is clear. Healing comes. Old wounds dissolve. Wellness and wholeness return.

The unseen miracle of God made this book possible. Some people do not think that they deserve a miracle-filled life. Miracles you want and are pleased that they occurred are seeking you. Your willingness to let miracles in is your willingness to let God in. God wants you to believe in your worthiness. Until you feel the love of God and the love of yourself, the joy of a miracle is between slim and none. You can realize when you have self-love. You will know contentment and peace despite your circumstances. Self-love is an unconditional experience no matter what is happening.

Nobody is exempt from being wounded in some way. Physically. Emotionally. Spiritually. Neglected.

Nobody can create a new past.

Everybody needs to let go of the past. Let go of your experience in a job where your body felt that you were dying a slow death. When you let go of your past timeline, you create space for something better. To experience the joy of a miracle, you must make space for it by letting go of what no longer serves you. Clear the clutter. And when you decide to embrace a new energy, your life can shift in an instant.

Everything that happened in your past and now had a reason. It is not just an accident that you are reading this book. Your soul led you here. You are being primed for your own miracle.

The Sacredness of the Human Body

People have failed to receive sensory impressions from the environment. People drift away from who they are. The world is without roots, without a feeling for history, without knowledge of the past. Church has never been helpful with its body-spirit ideas. Enjoyment and sensations become an illicit love affair. (Alexander Lowen, *The Betrayal of the Body*, pp. 1-18)

Lowen wrote, "A person experiences the reality of the world only through the body." Ibid., p. 5. If an individual is deprived of sensory stimulation for several weeks, she may hallucinate. William Schutz said, "Joy is the feeling that comes from the fulfillment of one's potential, and that person fulfills potential only to the degree that he or she is physically responsive to the world atmosphere." (William Schutz, *Joy: Expanding Human Awareness*, pp. 15-17)

Joy is the emotion of being alive. Joy is the receiving center for the environment's signals. There is a high degree of interrelatedness between sexuality and spirituality. (John Killinger, *Leave It to the Spirit*, pp. 59-61)

The world understands sexuality as an act between themselves unlike animals. Humans and animals have the same bodily needs. Humans have a soul that radically changes how intimacy is fully present in human lives. Human beings express themselves through the body. There is a huge difference between the brute satisfaction of the sexual instinct in most animals. Humans formally connect through marriage, where the tender, spiritual, loving, and joy are experienced. If people do not understand and fully experience this gift from God.

Love is mutual. Love grows as we become fully united in body and soul. Knowing the spiritual character of sexuality develops into a source of the deepest joy. (Alice Von Hildebrand, *By Love Refined*, pp. 37-38)

The prolonged, unnatural repression of the body and sexual tendencies during the act of worship has according to psychological research, a loss of the sense of reality in worship. Christians have been afraid of making real contact with the body, even when we shake hands, touch arms, hug, or greet each other with a holy kiss. Foot washing calls for washing each other's feet in warm, soapy water, rubbing salt over them, rinsing the feet, and then massaging them with oil.

The body communicates with more than the mouth and brain. Holy Spirit filled worship involves taste with the tongue. Smelling with the nose. Feeling with hands. The church has expressed an attitude of fear and distrust. They have evaluated the human mind as good and the body as evil. The flesh must be kept in obedience to the intellect. Harvey Cox said, "It is a mistake to try to defend jazz and modern dance by pretending that they are not sensuous and that therefore it is perfectly safe to allow them in church. They are sensuous and they are not safe." (Harvey Cox, *The Feast of Fools*, pp. 124-137)

Cox's attitude further contributes to misunderstanding and the silence of the church. In 2017, I wrote *The Silence of the Church: The Spiritual Struggle with Sexuality*. The sound of silence is the easy way to approach the human struggle with sexuality. Churches can create an atmosphere to talk about everything else, but not about "that." Many congregations are saying by this attitude that church is not a safe place to talk about our sexual selves.

Fear and shame head up the reason church leaders act out of knowing nothing to do.

During my Spiritual Visionquests for Joy, I run into many roadblocks. One would think church people would eagerly ask for help to bring the light of the gospel of grace and love. This silence of the church is crippling family life. As we look at the members of churches, we realize the need for dealing with the desires natural to our bodies. (James McReynolds, *The Silence of the Church: The Spiritual Struggle with Sexuality*, p. 13-14)

Younger people would not agree. They would rather dance than eat. The urge to dance is the basic part of human beings. We all tend to nod or move our bodies at symphony or country music concerts. We closely relate to expressions like "dancing to another tune" or "dancing for joy." A University of Nebraska graduate danced her way back to her seat after she received her diploma.

The Westminster Catechism begins with celebration: "The chief end of humankind is to love God and to enjoy God forever." The body becomes carefree in joy. Celebration is not part of most vents. We have forgotten the joy of ecstatic celebration. Scripture tells us, "The joy of the Lord is our strength." Without a joyful spirit of festivity, disciple becomes dull, not demonstrated with uninhibited gaiety and gratitude. Joy keeps everything moving. Joy produces bodily energy.

Singing a style or kind of music, or being in a preferred group, or sitting stoic throughout worship keeping the body from moving with delight. Body movements and modern spiritual dance are hidden. Children cannot help celebrating by dancing. See visions with the eyes Dream dreams. Use your gifts of intuition and imagination to demonstrate a flood of bodily feelings as fun and as joy.

The body is designed to move, to dance with delight. If we do not move our bodies, the bodies will soon not be capable of moving at all. There must be a healthy reason people in their old age keep on doing the polka.

Chapter Nine

Scattering Joy

Joy has woven itself into the tapestry of my soul. I professed my faith at age eight during Vacation Bible School at Woodlawn Baptist Church in Bristol, Tennessee. I felt full of joy after I walked home from my baptism. I sang "Joy to the World" in complete abandonment.

Joy has the power to alter the expression of genes throughout the brain and body, turning joy on and off that lower the amount of physical and emotional stress we normally experience throughout our day.

Pleasure chemicals such as dopamine are released. The brain can help your body relax and feel the joy.

Living Your Dream

Finding God's call, dedicating your life to it, and sharing the fruits of your experiences with others is our life's mission. Pursue your path with arms wide open. There are signposts pointing you to that place of passion. Denying any part of your self makes us feel empty and hopeless. We can find the path and becoming something, you never thought possible. The result of a sense of gratitude is to spread the joy to every soul you encounter. Raise your hand imagining your giving energy to somebody who needs it. Send energy from an experience of joy for which you are thankful. All life is connected. We need to be willing to be surprised when dreams come true such as the exposure of the ministry of this book.

Sharing your life is important. The world will give you feedback. Exposure of your creation will be as important as getting better at your work. If preaching or teaching is part of your vision, one goal is to let the Holy Spirit bring it into as many possibilities and situations that are possible.

Love is inseparable from service.

Love is the force that motivates us to give ourselves, to make sacrifices, to spend extra moments with sick friends, and to reach into our pockets for the poor. Love is an energy current that flows through us when we treat people decently and assure them of our concern. The Holy Spirit shakes us out of our self-centeredness and sets our souls on fire with love.

Sharing your dream with the world helps you understand how to create better. It might even cause to be alert to how you communicate including your thoughts in books. Gratitude is an antidote to moral apathy and spiritual indifference. We enjoy being around grateful people. Joy creeps into our open souls. We are joy. We exude joy and that is the miraculous cause that draws other people toward us.

This divine joy remains dormant until you take the agency to express it. As you become accustomed to certain aspects of your life usually means you are not mindful of them. Feeling joy enables your soul to discover everlasting springs of joy. Joy is your passion, your vision, your dreams, and life goals. Joy causes you to feel most fulfilled and flourishing. Each human being fulfils some purpose that each one and only that person has to offer the world. You are simply amazing. Talented. Rare. Gifted. Beautiful. Unique. Delicate treasure.
Irreplaceable. Priceless. Precious. Make the commitment to cherish and appreciate yourself.

The more joy we radiate the more joy comes back to us. Gratitude instantly connects us to everything and opens a continuing flow. One of our spiritual disciplines is to travel beyond emotional responses to life to a natural inclination of thankfulness. We work to become beacons of joy and love.

Become joy in the moment. If you enjoy writing, then write. Establish an intention at the start of the day to have experiences to reflect on. In my years of research on joy, I have discovered that discussing positive experiences leads to well-being, increased satisfaction, and even more energy. A wave of joy splashes over you.

Sharing joy causes us to re-experience joy and undoubtedly, we spread joy to another. My wife Laurel gives genuine commendation each year by buying loaves of tasty bread for every single member. It proves to be a motivating cheer up.

Each next moment is improved by the love in the present. Progress leads to purpose. Pursuing purpose leads to progress. Love makes it possible to connect our journey to outer accomplishments unless we find motivation to link with God in intimate union. We also discover communion with those entrusted to our care. Without love, friendship and family fall apart.

Nobody's dream is as grand as who we become by the effort required to be in sync with your purpose. Life situations change quickly. We learn to adjust nimbly to the changing landscape in the journey of life. This part of your timeline of life will never be experienced again. Invite joy to live with you and go where you live. (M.
Eid and E. Diener, "Norms for Experiencing Emotions in Different Cultures," *Journal of Personality and Social Psychology*, 81, 2001, pp. 869-885

Enjoy the journey. Cherish every time your publisher sends you galleys for your book. Enjoy the writer's trips in all the highs and lows. Where we are now is where life unfolds. Enjoy the preparation as much as the result.

My grandson Ethan Coffin gave me a plaque several years ago that read, "Find joy in the journey." Make today count. Enjoy and celebrate how far you have come, and those lessons and experiences along the way. Thanksgiving opens our souls fully with the joy that is ours at any given moment.

When we reach the destination of our life on earth, we must remember to enjoy every aspect. That is, we remember to love and express love for those whom we hold dear, and all the things that we appreciate.

Joy of Sharing Joy

Appreciation of our joy draws our attention to positive experiences. Joy grows when we share it. Pleasure has no relish unless we share it. People who shared their positive experiences knew a boost in their well-being than those who did not share.

Research indicates that nearly three times more positive experiences happen in a day than negative. Some let the negative take over and ruin the day. We are reluctant to share the positive. Why? Guilt. Undeserving. Humility.

Regularly shared happiness and joy over a long period of time brings a zest of life and a high level of energy. For more than 50 years, my sharing about joy has keep me in focus about joy and life. Sharing my joys increases my joy. Telling others about our joy has far greater benefits than just remembering it. We can help others' joy by encouraging them to share their must positive experiences. Albert Schweitzer, German missionary, musician, and physician observed, "Joy is the only thing that multiplies when you share it."

The promise of joy blares at us from political platforms, commercials for most anything on televisions. If we buy the right cereal, the right automobile, the right toothpaste, deodorant, or shaving cream, we will discover joy.

Pleasure is another commodity that the world seeks. Old people want the right cable channels. We choose fast food for meals. We drink, eat, and make love s we yearn for joy. Joy is so much wide than our world. Preaching from Paul's letter to the Philippians, we share the joy that comes from being grasped by God is wider than anything pushed upon us by the world. Joy is influenced by circumstances, but it does not depend on them. The troubles of Paul presented him with options of despair, but he chose joy.

Joy comes to us when we realize that all things happen for a reason, the pleasant as well as the painful. Joy wraps us in the embrace of a God whose presence is the prime occasion for joy. Joy is not something we achieve. Joy is a gift. Thanksgiving is not an insurance policy, never a guaranteed appointment as Catholics, Episcopalians, or Methodists may take for granted. Gratitude is a natural response to a miracle of life. The mysterious dynamics of living in joy is that everything needed is there all the time. When we talk about positive things happening in our lives, we are validating them. Sharing joy will open our eyes to the support system. Those around us will see their spirits lifted.

Ron James summarizes the distinctive emotion of joy. He writes, "To speak of joy one has to speak about the capacity of the soul to be apprehended, to be grasped by beauty, by love, by mystery, by God, by that which is beyond us and addresses us at the level of our soul, requiring our surrender if ever we would know its promise or search the depths of our longing." (Ron James, *A Joy Wider Than the World: A Teaching and Preaching Commentary on Philippians*, p.7)

Everybody has a right to joy.

Joy is simple. Nobody must think about it. We feel it. We are surprised by it. We feel joy in our bodies. We see it on faces throughout the world. It is easy to identify people experiencing joy. Bright eyes. Laughter. Smiles. Upright poster. As I travel the world, I speak English when I share joy. Joy has a universal language. We encounter joy every time we encounter delight. Joy can't be faked or conjured up. Real smiles are not in conscious control. Joy is automatic. Joy is visceral. Joy is an essential and intrinsic part of the mind. Joy is universally within everyone. Joy is the birthright of every human being.

Encounters with Christ leads to conversion. The witness of a joy-filled and Spirit filled life attracts others. The joy of the Christian life stands out. We hear this repeatedly. "They have something I want, but I do not have." To be effective in sharing good news, we must communicate the heart of the gospel. We were all created to be amazing. Being ourselves with the Spirit, we can set the world on fire. Salvation is a gift. It is offered to each person. Before this gift can be owned, it must be accepted. This decision to accept God's gift, we must decide and make the choice to become a disciple of Jesus. We experience renewal.

Joy is not just the result of a positive experience. It is a propulsive force towards more positivity. Even in nations where their citizens are living in dire circumstances, people seek out moments of delight. Their joys are not irrational impulses. Joy moments give respite from their hardship and offer hope for the future. Visual beauty elicits pride and self-esteem and bridge social and political gaps. Delightful and fun times, even in the poorest of countries, is a profound need. (Isen, Albert M., "Success, Failure, Attention, and Reaction to Others: The Warm Glow of Success," *Journal of Personality and Social Psychology*, 15, 1999, pp. 294-301)

Notes from the Author's Sermons on Joy

Some quotes include: "Christian Joy is a good feeling in the soul, produced by the Holy Spirit, as the spirit causes us to see the beauty of Christ in the word and in the world." John Piper.

"The inward peace and sufficiency that is not affected by outward circumstances." Warren Wiersbe.

"This is what binds all people and all creation together, the gratuity of the gift of being." Matthew Fox.

"Joy is the response and reaction of the soul to the knowledge of the Lord Jesus Christ." Martin Lloyd-Jones.

During a local church vision quest, I used II Corinthians 10:5. The points were:

1. Notice negative thoughts. 2. Reject negative thoughts. 3. Replace negative thoughts.

If you are ready to be rescued, God is ready to pull you out of the muck of negativity and discouragement.

Joy is in the Lord for salvation. Read Psalm 40:16, 51:12. For God's help. Psalm 63:7. For God's Word. Psalm 119:111. Joy is in the Lord. Isaiah 9:3. Joy is in the incarnation. Luke 1:44, John 15:11, Mathew 2:10-11. Joy for today. John 16:16-22, Philippians 4:4-13. I have collected thousands of quotes on joy.

Some of the questions I have used in counseling and prayer meetings: How would you define joy? Who are people in your life that have joy? How do you know they have joy? What often steals your joy? What do you think God is asking you to do through your being filled with the Holy Spirit who gives you the fruit of the spirit including joy? I find joy-seeking in many congregations that are alive with joy.

Church Street United Methodist Church

Church Street is in Knoxville, Tennessee. In a 2022 newsletter, they urged their members to seek joy. Church Street is the largest and most impactful congregation in the Holston Conference of the United Methodist Church. The editor wrote, "It is far too easy to get stuck in the weeds in these days. If we are not careful, we forget to look around and celebrate the good things that are all around.

"Seeking joy is not turning a blind eye to pain or ignoring the hard things in our lives and world. That is why we make room for grief. Seeking joy is about opening our eyes to the grace that sustains and delights during our ordinary lives.

"Today's resource is a simple practice; one we have talked about. We call it gratitude journaling. You could call it something else. Thankful list. Joy sightings. The concept is simple. Challenge yourself to document the things that bring you joy each day. Here are some ways to practice. Take a photo everyday of something joyful. Write down three things each night that you are thankful for. Share around the dinner table your favorite parts of the day. Start each morning by saying a thank you prayer for the things that bring you joy.

"This is not an exhaustive list. It is merely a starting place. This practice can be tweaked to fit your life in a multitude of ways. Make it your own. Whenever I am conceitedly practicing this, I am always surprised by the way my mind is transformed. I start to see joy popping up all around, even in the most unexpected places.

"There is joy to be found. I believe that with my whole heart and honestly, I think seeking joy while we are walking through darkness is one of the ways that we become more like Jesus.

"Let us seek joy. This simple act might just change everything."

Advent: Reflecting on the Theme of Joy at Baylor University

Baylor University is a Baptist university. In 2021, they celebrated each week of Advent. Ronald Angelo Johnson of the Department of History said, "One of the harder parts of my Christian journey is yielding to God's will when I already have a plan. When things seem fine in my life, why does God need to complicate them?"

Burt Burleson, D. Min., related concerning "Joy as a Poetic Paradox." "God beyond us is God with us, Yahweh, and Emmanuel. God almighty, the vulnerable swaddled baby, are one and the same, so large, and brilliant, tiny, and tender."

Angela Gorrell who teaches at the George W. Truett Theological Seminary, housed at Baylor said, "Joy has grit. It does not break easily. Joy can stare life's most brutal moments down and live, because it is made and sustained by those things that always remain, even when we cannot see them—truth, meaning, beauty, goodness, and connection to God."

Gracie Kellner, student body president at Baylor reflected, "Whether you feel like you are in a time of waiting, suffering, or hopelessness, do not lose sight of the ultimate source of joy: Jesus."

Horace J. Maxile of the Baylor School of Music said: "Joy is a resolute delight. When hope reaches beyond creation and resides with the Creator, seedlings of joy may well take root and sprout." Maxile also said, "Joy is our delight. 'This joy I have, the world didn't give me. The world didn't give it. The world cannot take it away.' This praise chorus is one I have sung since my childhood, and its message becomes even more clear as I grow older. As with certain praise choruses from black vernacular musical traditions and contemporary performance practices, words can be substituted to create dynamic and expressive trajectories.

"When hope reaches beyond creation and resides with the Creator. I believe a joyous existence and persistence allows us to see such acts of grace in our own lives, even when they may not be readily apparent on the surface.

"People, events, and circumstances might make us happy. They may even confirm the goodness and grace of the Source of our joy. This joy springs from hopes on things eternal and causes us to reflect on such things and the awesome gift of Christ. I have heard some preachers say that happiness is based on happenings, but joy comes from the inside. This joy fuels my gifts and talents, and it is my strength,

"May we find rest in this joy, this peace, and share some of the same with others in this season as well as the days, months, and years that follow. Joy is truly a humbling gift." (Bulletin from the Baylor Religious Hour for week three of advent 2021)

Therapeutic Preaching

Preaching is proclamation of the good news that God has redeemed the world through Christ in the power of the Holy Spirit. Fosdick said that preaching was counseling from the pulpit. My book, *The Joy of Preaching*, I attempt to suggest the right way to craft a sermon. Preaching is encountering Jesus through the Word of God. My colleague at Vanderbilt, Harold Bales, said my book was a helpful guide. Cathy Stander, my dear pastor friend in Louisville, Nebraska, wrote a second forward, "I remember Jim and his joy for being chosen to preach God's Word and after seeking forgiveness, I am lifted up and find it a joy to preach."

Hans Urs von Balthasar, an Australian professor of preaching, names his preaching "Christocentric therapeutic oral communication." It is natural to turn to his sermons in search of another helpful example of effective preaching. My mentor, John Killinger, is the best preacher I know. Dr.

Killinger in his printed sermons shows how preaching and pastoral counseling involve the same fundamental pastoral moves.

As a licensed mental health practitioner, I did psychotherapy with many children, youth, and adults who I diagnosed as dealing with "generalized anxiety disorder." Many ministers have fit this category. Some have lost their joy and are standing apart from Jesus and his offer of blessedness. My calling in teaching, counseling, writing, and preaching is for humans to receive eternal life and salvation as gifts from God. Another part is to embrace the positive meaning in suffering. And a third part is communicating your joy in Christ to the world.

One of my courses at Vanderbilt Divinity School was on the preaching and counseling life of Harry Emerson Fosdick, the famed pastor of the Riverside Church, an American Baptist, and United Church of Christ congregation in New
York. Our professor taught us the seminal work of therapeutic preaching by Fosdick and his early followers. We did a review of Fosdick's project of offering "counseling on a group scale."

In presenting various critiques of the Riverside pastor's homiletic approach, the solution for the problem was that therapeutic preaching needs to be thoroughly theological. Falbus Landry, a Christian Church (Disciples of Christ) ordained minister, taught the course. Students reflected on the theological diagnosis that accounts for so much anxiety. Harry Emerson Fosdick's group counseling approach is a source for preaching. Fosdick's approach gained much attention among American Protestant preachers in the twentieth century.

Fosdick recalls that what planted the seed of his new approach to preaching was a pastoral counseling experience with a young man "from one of the church's finest families, who lived in the grip of alcoholism. (Harry E. Fosdick, "Personal Counseling and Preaching," *Pastoral Psychology*, 1952, pp. 11-17)

For Fosdick preaching the saving gospel of Christ is addressing real problems, aiming the message at an individual need. The expectation is that lives will be transformed and restored. Fosdick insisted that it is not a matter of coming up with a novel and intriguing topic for the sermon. It was to focus the mind on real needs of people. Preaching has the power to bring renewal and healing to confused and suffering persons. "The preacher should go into his pulpit expecting that lives will be made over, families will be saved, young people will be directed into wholesome paths, potential suicides will become joyful and useful members of society, and doubters will become vibrant believers." (*Ibid.*, p. 16)

Fosdick's focus on joy illustrates his method. He begins by contending that the preacher should not start with the joy of the fourth or fifth century. Focus on the concrete difficulties that people face as they attempt to live joyfully. A helpful sermon is not simply a conversation about joy. It goes much further and produces joy.

Fosdick insisted that "all powerful preaching is creative. It brings to pass in the lives of the congregation the thing it talks about." (*Ibid.*, p. 16) The joy of preaching is that it has the power to transform and restore. Preaching that is faithful to the gospel must be done by one who is "filled with the spirit." Riverside's congregation should have majored on the Holy Spirit to bring the fruit of the Spirit that includes joy.

To set the scene for my joy of preaching, I reflect on the situational and historical factors that led to anxiety in the modern world. Life for many feels uncertain and insecure. The world has a futility and meaninglessness associated by the experience of being left out of a machine that we have no control over.

The world's people feel trapped. The ultimate cause is our failure to unite with Christ. All pervasive deep joy is the gift that Christ offers to the world. When a person is filled with the Holy Spirit, she will experience joy that discovers life in all its difficulties, reversals, rejections, and disappointments, is ultimate working for our good. Being in the Holy Spirit through faith in self-giving. God gives the special gift of joy. Joy is a gift of love that is the eternal blessedness of God. In giving humans eternal love and joy, God gives the gift of a share in the eternal, blessed life of God.

Like the two shots and a booster to prevent covid-19 deaths, the pure joy comes from the grace of God can be relied on to ward off sickness wrapped in hopelessness and meaninglessness. The joy in Christ that is so generously and lovingly given is meant to be shared with the world. Joy shared with others is joy magnified. Divine action and grace, not human wisdom, is the focus for sharing "the joy of the Lord."

Receive your life and salvation as the gift from God. Embrace the positive meaning in suffering. Communicate your joy to the world.

Joy ministers forget the Great Commission and the global identification for sharing the joy of the Lord. Trips to other nations will not display your passion for offering the joy of salvation. Travel has enlightened my understanding and my surprising impact.

Joy increases through evangelism.

God delights to multiply our joy by calling us into the fields of evangelism. The seventy-two that Jesus sent experienced this joy first-hand. Joy increases through evangelism because we experience God at work. Read Luke 10. Those who engage in ministry know the joy in the lives of individuals, churches, and communities. Telling or writing to others about the grace of God reminds us of the love of God. The joy of Jesus made a profound impression on his disciples. Faithful evangelism of pastors, congregations, and denominations always leads to more fulness of God.
The disciples would never forget how their joy increased through laboring in his name. Luke listened to the disciples' experience and included in his gospel of joy.

The United States and the United Kingdom now has become spiritually powerless. People are now leaving the organized formal churches. Globally, millions of people find joy in Jesus and his church. Recent research showed that nearly three billion people will identify themselves as Christians in 2023. I shared my vision for joy in Kenya in the 1980s. Daniel Mbai was a collogue student at Midwestern Baptist Theological Seminary in Kansas City. Danny was well-liked. He did not understand how racism could be so prevalent in the United States. One weekend, Danny shared in a revival at Kingsville Baptist Church in Kingsville, Missouri.
My congregation responded with kindness and acceptance. His skin was very dark. He asked various people if they had ever heard an African preacher. Danny and I slept in the same bed together. We enjoyed food and drink. In the two years I knew him, we loved to go to the awesome Kansas City restaurants. Danny is a high government official in Kenya today.

One of the reasons I think Danny came into my life was to enable me to understand African culture. His insights made me want to make missionary trips to the nations of Africa, 50 in all, that I have been privileged to take during my efforts to share God's joy with so many. After I preached in one congregation near Nairobi, and we started to travel to the next town where we were going to eat a meal and spend the night. Danny and his friend Moses Jacobi had only been to that locality one other time. The three of us walked the whole way. We shared in joyous fellowship. I notice the evening son was getting lower and lower. I could see nothing but the African countryside. We just keep walking. The late afternoon sun had a bring orange and red color. The sun dipped below the horizon. As it became a deep purple, we kept on walking and talking. Then it was pitch black. I was walking in the middle of an African forest. I was listening to sounds that I had never heard before. The nocturnal animals were coming out.

We had now waked twenty miles. I was exhausted. Danny and Moses were still full of energy. I was moved to preach about life as a journey. On a journey, we do not know exactly where we are going. We have never traveled that way. I trusted my friend Danny and Moses. I never knew what was around the next bend. Heck, we couldn't even see the next coming bend. God had called us to this journey. We were all of us created in the image of God. The trip had immense proportions. Eternal proportions. Connecting proportions. Infinite proportions. Joyful proportions.

The world has not given the people in Kenya or in any third world nation much joy. Most are frustrated. They do not have simple things they need like water, food, and shelter. It is harder for them to choose joy. Joy is a continuous commitment. Traveling as a college student home summer missionary is not the same as going where you are the minority. My sermons were translated into Spanish in my 1962 mission to New Mexico. International ministry is not the same. Printing of books and Bibles becomes an impossibility. The Bible has not yet been translated into many African languages.

Printing of Bibles

Printing of Bibles will total 100 million in the world in 2023. Only five billion were printed in 1910. Today almost 1.9 billion Bibles are in circulation in the world. Bill Firebaugh, a neighbor and high school friend in Bristol, Tennessee serves as a missionary and Bible translator in the Philippines.

If joy is inside of every human as an aspect of being. Joy has existed for as long as humans have existed. Scientific research has proved that human life was created in Africa. The origin of joy lies within the origin of humanity. People in many nations feel stuck like a hamster on a wheel. Life becomes dull and boring. They run on fumes. They are anxious and scattered to the winds. They feel a disconnection from themselves and from God.

The evolution of technology and industrial advancements have had an impact on the decline of joy that we perceive as we travel to other countries. Joy is disguised everywhere as something we must look for outside ourselves. People acquire the stuff that we have been told will create a joyful life. Joy can never be realized in shinier, bigger, better, and sparkler things. Joy is not a means to an end. We humans are the origin of joy. When Dr. Chris Meadows said, "Joy does not come from the things we do. It flows from inside us." Joy is an internal experience. It is not an external experience. Joy is being present and enjoying what we have, where we are living, whatever you find yourself doing, and however we share joy with the world. Joy is inside everyone. Joy is international.

Becoming ministers of joy to the world is a movement. This movement is beginning to be discussed in every corner of the earth. Joy is our choice. Nobody can ever take it away. When I hear a person sharing a joy, I often tear up. I find so much joy in other people's miracles. It increases my appreciation for life.
This book is a joy jumpstart, a guided journey to rediscover what makes us full of life. Readers, you deserve a vibrant, joyful life. The world attempts to say that joy does not matter. This ministry is my purpose. It is my badge of honor. Joy inspires me. I feel less anxiety and weakness. Joy energizes me.

The whole world has been greatly blessed with the prolific writings of my friend John Killinger. In his devotional guide the gospel of Luke, his book title is "*The Gospel of Contagious Joy*. Ernest Campbell, former pastor of the Riverside Church in New York, wrote, "Killinger doesn't simply tell us about the good life. He makes us want to live it." (John Killinger, *A Devotional Guide to Luke: The Gospel of Contagious Joy*, back cover)

Kent Keith wrote an inspiring poem called "The Paradoxical Commandments." My loving wife Laurel used it to inspire her nurses when she served more than twenty years as the Director of Nursing at the Dialysis Center of Lincoln, Nebraska.

"People are illogical, unreasonable, and self-centered.
        Love them anyway.
If you do good, people will accuse you of selfish ulterior motives.
        Do good anyway.

If you are successful, you will win false friends and true enemies.
　　Succeed anyway.
The good you do today will be forgotten tomorrow.
　　Do it anyway.
Honesty and frankness make you vulnerable.
　　Be honest and frank anyway.
The biggest men and women with the biggest ideas can be shot down
by the smallest men and women with the smallest minds.
　　Think big anyway.
People favor underdogs but follow only top dogs.
　　Fight for a few underdogs anyway.
What you spend years building may be destroyed overnight.
　　Build anyway.
People really need help but may attack you if you do help them.
　　Help people anyway.
Give the world the best you have, and you'll get kicked in the teeth.
Give the world the best you have anyway.

(Kent M. Keith, *Anyway: The Paradoxical Commandments*, pp. 15-18)

Keith's book is about the grace, wisdom, and joy that come from facing the worst in the world with the best in ourselves. The challenge is to do what is right and good, even if others give you no appreciation.

Simple People Respond

Dmitri in The Brothers Karamazov says that God will be kept alive in the prisons if not allowed to die among the intellectuals and respectable people. This insight has always been the truth. The simple people, the outcasts, the little people understand and respond to the call of God when God is neglected in finer circles. (John Killinger, *Day by Day with Jesus*, pp. 114-115)

For us to reject fellow believers is like rejecting our blood relatives. We might not like them, but the ties of blood are always there. Our souls are loving those outcasts, the little people, binding us together. To reject another is to reject ourselves. It is rejecting our brothers and sisters.

Conversion to Jesus Christ is a struggle with love and self-recognition. Jesus is the gospel of joy to me about myself. The double desire is to love and be loved is common to every human being. All our desires spring from the same source. Even when our desires are misdirected, erratic, and destructive these relate to the love of God. We all share this impulse toward love as we understand it. That impulse reveals the limitations and the possibilities of a particular time or place. Our inner compass knows more than we do. Romans 8:28. We are all extremely vulnerable. When we love another person, we either want to merge with them, or put-up barriers to keep them out.

It is the simple part of each of us that follows you. That also means the simple part will never stop willingly coming after God. Another part will chase illusions and phantoms. (*Ibid.*, p. 115)

Jesus commands us to share abundantly as the kingdom of joy springs up in response to the broadcasting of the gospel of joy in most unlikely places. Read Mark 4:26-29. Our ministry of joy concerns the joyous abandonment with which a farmer does her work. She broadcasts the seed, then goes about her daily chores. The grain appears without her knowing it. That was my reaction as God created vast exposure to my own proclaiming of the gospel of joy through my writing books.
The kingdom of God sows miraculous seed, Seeds coming up are indeed miracles. We need not spend our energy and time asking what happened to cause the seed to take root. We can relax and be concerned for the harvest.

That is the vision quest of this writer and his publisher and the readers. Our beginnings have been humble. I pray for an incredible harvest capable of sheltering believers from all nations. The kingdom of God is like the mustard seed.

We find courage from Jesus' teachings. Let God bless you with the gospel of joy. God blesses our tiny and weak efforts. The mustard seed was such an effective illustration. It was so small and yet produced such a towering bush. The bushes were ten to twelve feet tall, and they were thirty feet around in circumference. In scattering joy through preaching, the minister is communicating in her own personality. If she is a free woman and if this freedom is expressed in the style she uses, her preaching will have the effect of setting other people free for living in joy.

The Church of joy must gain wisdom to apply biblical truth to the realities of life. Ministers and missionaries affiliated with sharing the gospel of joy at home or internationally abroad must be undergirded to expound salvation.

We are the church, the source of joy, kindness, and compassion. Our task is to bring light into the dark world.

Let nothing prevent us from envisioning the refugees from the Middle East, Asia, and Africa, the starving of India and South America, the poor throughout the world including Europe and the United States of America.

We must scatter strong faith, overcome petty divisions, deepen worship, and intimate prayer, couple love with justice, magnify Jesus the Christ, both now and forever.

Chapter Ten

Discipline and Joy

Joy involves discipline as we maintain joy. Root your joy in the standing you have in Christ. If you believe joy is dependent on circumstances, it will not remain. Look inward and outward, and upward. Renew joy by embracing the promise of salvation. Maintaining joy is a spiritual discipline. Each evening before we go to sleep, we can discipline ourselves to visualize us finding the keys to joy. Work to create visual reminders to keep our souls focused on a positive direction. Work as if your joy depends on you. Pray as if it depends on God. Discipline leads us to a deeper inner life. This leads us into an overwhelming joy.

There are undisciplined, unprincipled, and opportunistic people who take advantage of our eagerness and gullibility. Discipline is the quiet and consistent way we do the will of God. (John Killinger, *Day by Day with Jesus*, pp. 32-33)

The spiritual fruit of patience is not easy. In the definition of love in I Corinthians 13 begins, "Love is patient." Patience is not the ability to wait. It is keeping a joy attitude while we wait. Patience means enduring hardship. Patience means perseverance. Growing in grace is growing in patience. Read James 1:19-20. Being slow to speak involves learning when to speak. Just as conversion and salvation take time for completion, the path to patience is long in time.

The Quaker Richard Foster wrote a classic book about disciplines. Quakers use meditation. Prayer. Fasting. Study. Simplicity. Solitude. Submission. Service. Confession. Worship. Guidance. Celebration. D. Elton Trueblood said that discipline can free us from habits that take away our joy and intimacy with God. Trueblood taught at a Quaker college in Indiana. His messages during Religious Focus Week in 1962 at Carson-Newman College, are still part of my guidance that has had to be restored from time to time.

The Archbishop of Canterbury, then Donald Coggan, said, "I go through life as a transient on his way to eternity, made in the image of God but with that image debased, needing to be taught, how to meditate, to worship, to think."

Every church congregation is unique. The miraculous diversity in the people is inspiring. Countless factors are involved: cultural norms, gender, personality, ethnicity, structure, unexpected events. The most authoritative statement ever made was from Jesus. Read Matthew 28:18-20. Jesus is God. (Curtis Martin, *Making Missionary Disciples*, pp. 38-39)

A rarely read theologian named John Woolman advised, "It is good for thee to dwell deep, that thou mayest feel and understand the spirits of people." (John Woolman, *The Journal of John Woolman*, p. 118)

Joy is the keynote of all discipline. We long for God. Read Psalm 42:1-2, 7. Souls long to launch out into the deep. We cannot restore our own souls by giving into our own wills. Willpower will not do. Our dint of will makes a satisfied showing for a brief time, but son reveals the true condition. We do not intentionally explode with anger. We betray our inner selves by our eyes. Hands. Tongue. Chin. Body. Words. (Richard Foster, *Celebration of Discipline*, pp. 4-5)

We have free will and we are architects of how we discipline ourselves. We must be disciplined to continue to see every problem from a clearer perspective. Write to God in your journal to ask for guidance. Stay true to the voice of God. Intuitive nudges, messages, or feelings will ooze into our best self. We get to busy to act on this divinely guided support. We must trust that inner voice. Inner righteousness is a gift from God. Only God can work from the inside. God has given disciplines as a means of receiving grace.

I cherish my ministry as an elder in the United Methodist Church. Methodists often communicate the purpose of our sanctification. This theological term means to let the Spirit work to conform us to the image of Jesus. That calling is not merely an individual one. It is for every family, every church, every activity throughout life.

Take time to get centered and focused. Create your own daily ritual. Begin feeling that you gain more joy and excitement over what the day holds for us. When we care for ourselves, we are more balanced and centered. We share the best we are out into the world.

Joyful people need a quiet time. This discipline is worth every second. Each morning I fix a cup of tea and I eat a yogurt. I walk into my home office. I silently turn on the light. I sit my body into a comfortable chair. I begin with a prayer that God will teach me the ways of God. I pick up my Bible and open it. I breath in the glory of God's presence. God meets me in the little corner of my office. God can talk with me before the Nebraska sun shows its face out my window among the trees in the park in front of my house.

I pray through names on my current prayer list. I pray for situations that need a touch from God. Life is busy. Life is wonderful. Discover God's purpose for you. We are all more than ordinary. We have a divine nature. Never compare your uniqueness to others. When we understand and appreciate the gifts from God, then we experience joy. Quiet yourself to recognize the hand of God upon your life. Joy is not the absence of pain, but it is the presence of God. Discipline brings internal changes. Joy-filled souls experience an inner transformation.

Share joy every day. Simple interactions build your character, faith, and testimony. Include new people into your circle of friends. Look for God in the ordinary.

The discipline of selfless service connects us to other humans in a primal way. Every day brings opportunities to perform simple acts of service. The discipline of a spiritual pioneer is to attain union with God. Unconditional acts of service have the power to raise consciousness of the receiver and the giver. True and confident servants are drawn to small service because she sees it as important. Ambitious ministers require external rewards. Results. Reciprocation. Disciplined ministers are satisfied with receiving the low places. They have no need to calculate results. Their call is not temporary, but the soul of a called minister sometimes requires waiting. The grace of humility is worked into our lives with the grace of humility. Service is the most conducive to humility. Read I John 2:16.

Joy Gives Us Freedom.

The discipline in joy will give us freedom. Even though we might think that discipline and times of restoration, we must keep this in mind. Discipline is the path to emotional and spiritual freedom. Instead of making us tense or anxious, disciple sets us up for calm and peace.

Discipline yourself to create a private sanctuary in your home. Condition both mind and body to meditate. Wrap yourself in the grace of God. Move into your sacred place for quiet reflection that inspires divine union and peace. Once we have conquered our minds, we have conquered the world. Finding joy and beauty within, the entire world becomes infused with this joy.

Instead of seeing our experiences or encounters with others as random experiences, we see them as deliberate, spiritual events that remind us of who we are. Our souls are being disciplined by sacred hands. Jesus presented radical social teaching. He totally reversed the contemporary definition of greatness. His idea about greatness was to become a servant of all. Jesus' life was living in joy which was an entire new order of leadership. Read Mark 8:34, 9:35.

E. Stanley Jones served as a missionary for Methodists. He tells of an African man, who following his conversion and his profession of faith changed his name to After. His life had become disciplined "after" his conversion.

The process of spiritual awakening is a life-long journey. This process is without any predetermined destination. God's grace will lead us down our own unique pathway. Once we begin replacing old beliefs with new ones, it becomes even more important to use our intuition to determine what we do next. Putting too much stock in someone else's view of what we should do is a certain way to prevent spirit inspired insights. Divine energy is available to each one of us to support the plan for our living. It is helpful to get input from people we respect. It is far more important to develop a strong connection with our own intelligence, our own inner guidance system, especially we are beginning to discipline ourselves to cocreate our lives with God.

The closer we come with God, the more we love. Our intimate relationships grow into miracles. A new restored life is disciplined with enthusiasm. Spiritual reading and prayer enable us to solve daily difficulties. The Holy Spirit and other people communicates that our struggles are shared with innumerable souls. Imperfections continue in our spiritual enthusiasm. Remember that flowers do not bloom at the same time. Love of God never diminish love for other important people.

Discipline brings the beauty of an intense spiritual life. We enjoy its delights. We also enjoy sharing the life on God now living inside us. (Alice von Hildebrand, *By Love Refined*, pp. 201-203)

When we are receptive to the influence of grace, we live life on a deeper level. Senses are heightened. We feel more. We appreciate the subtleties of life. We discover joy in simple things and in unexpected places. We have faith that all events are occurring as they should. We know we are connected, and that each one of us can choose joy. Henri Nouwen urged joy seekers to "be surprised by joy, be surprised by the little flower that shows its beauty in the midst of a barren desert and be surprised by the immense healing power that keeps bursting fort like springs of fresh water from the depths of our pain." (Henri L.M. Nouwen, *You Are the Beloved: Daily Meditations for Spiritual Living*, p. 92)

Joy is right in front of us undetected and undisciplined and undefined. Joy is not like security or prosperity. One second of disciplined joy is worth many hours of pleasure. In joy, we are aware of a deeper love and joy of God. The choice to serve and the choice to become a servant as we want to be in charge. We desire to be the one whom we will serve and when we will serve. Being available and vulnerable is what we pledge when we are ordained as ministers of word and sacrament.

William Wordsworth describes the shock and pain he felt the instant he turned to share an unexpecting moment of joy with a loved one who had died. (William Wordsworth, *Surprised by Joy: Poems*, p. 17)

"Joy does not simply happen to us," wrote Henri Nouwen. "We must choose joy and keep choosing it every day. It is a choice based on the knowledge that we belong to God and have found in God our refuge and our safety and that nothing, not even death, can take God from us." Henri Nouwen, *Ibid*, p. 169)

Being anointed as the minister of joy to the world, I understand the value of being kind and serving with common courtesy. To have the privilege, I never despise the rules of relationship which differ in every culture. Read Titus 3:2.

I do not dare to blunder into some small home or village demanding to be heard. Even if we share the gospel of joy in our own culture, we first undergo points of understanding. I first realized this truth when the associational missionary in New Mexico gave the summer missionaries insight on how to act and what not to say.
These disciplines including expressing gratitude and giving letters of appreciation. He told us that we were in the ministry of Jesus, not our own, and we must minister with a towel.

This orientation made me free to value people everywhere. It gave me clues to love people unconditionally. We give up expecting love in return. We will not anticipate being treated in a certain way. Our joy does not depend on getting what we want. Read Philippians 2:4. We live lives of simplicity that offers help when needed. Being in a joy, we perform small acts of kindness like sharing food, mowing a lawn, shoveling snow, taking time to visit, sharing our things. Nobody can do everything, but everybody can do something.

Our world is an independent international and connected place. Those who choose to be joyful are identified by both power and compassion. George Fox said, "Dwell in the life and love and power and wisdom of God. Be in unity with one another and with God." The discipline that gives us the joy of God is like scattered fire, flaming torches in the night. Read Philippians 3:14. Paul the apostle was fired up to press on toward the goal of the upward call of God in Christ Jesus."

That same challenge is ours now. I pray that my books on joy have sobered your assessment of where you are now. Serving as the minister of joy to the world, my commitment is to help you beyond the mire of doom and gloom that keeps us from intimacy with God. Intimacy with God, ourselves, and others cannot be rooted in human effort. Everything does happen for a reason. There are now almost eight billion people living with us on earth. We shall never know them all or even a tiny fraction. Joy wells up from within through the action of grace and our humble response.

Afterword

With this book, my dad, Dr. James McReynolds, enthusiastically continues his ministry of joy to the world. Through his ministry, he touches lives across the globe. In this book, my dad describes discovering that his works are available in many languages from online booksellers globally, learning through serendipitous discoveries, such as finding his own book in a quaint London bookstore, and indeed this message of joy that he shares freely benefits others around the world.

His expansive message has global reach, but it is based on finding meaning in small quiet moments, stillness, in the small voice, in solitude. My dad has taught me to seek joy in such quiet moments—and to find it—since I was a child.

We would walk together and pick up stones, turn them over, decipher markings, feel the smooth or rough texture. Together we would find the flat round stones. He patiently taught me which ones were best, how to curve my hand around the flat ones, look across the still surface of the water, and flick my wrist so the stone would fly parallel to the surface and skip across the water. These simple moments of stillness, walking along in nature with my dad, remain some of the most joyful memories of my life.

Later, as I faced difficult decisions—where to go to school, what job to take, where to live, whether to take on a responsibility—his advice would be and remains to "go where the joy is." Although we can find joy in our earthly lives, in the natural world, in the smile of a friend, my dad writes and believes that we can find eternal joy in living out God's plan for us. Rather than rush and run a race, caught in earthly ambition, my dad has taught and modeled for me that it is better to slow down, be still, and seek a joyful life of meaning and purpose.

In this book, and in his other works, my dad shows that joy is available to everyone, in the simple quiet times—a walk, a cup of tea, a sunset. We just need to "stop and notice the delightful wonders of life." I am grateful for all my dad has taught me by his example and thankful that his ministry of joy to the world continues to expand its global reach.

Linda McReynolds
Bethesda, Maryland

Appendix

In counseling as a joyologist, I use the following guidance to indicate opinions and experiences of joy in the past week.

In the past week, how often have you felt joy?

2	3	4	5	6	7
Not at all	Hardly at all	A few times	Several times.	Number of times	Often

In the past week, how often have you felt enthusiastic?

2	3	4	5.	6	7
Not at all	Hardly at all	A few times	Several Times	Number of times	Often

Because of the joy I experienced this week, time seemed to fly.

1	4	7
Completely agree	Neither agree nor disagree	Strongly agree

This week I found myself enjoying something so much I lost track of time.

1	4	7
Completely agree	Neither agree nor disagree	Strongly agree

This week I felt free.

1	4	7
Completely agree	Neither agree nor disagree	Strongly agree

This week, I felt ready to enjoy whatever opportunity presented itself.

1	4	7
Completely agree	Neither agree nor disagree	Strongly agree

7. Something happened this week that made me feel like celebrating.

1	4	7
Completely agree	Neither agree nor disagree	Strongly agree

8. This week the reality of my life was as it should be.

1	4	7
Completely agree	Neither agree nor disagree	Strongly agree

9. This week I felt free to play.

1	4	7
Completely agree	Neither agree nor disagree	Strongly agree

10. This week my life went well, and it made sense to me.

1	4	7
Completely agree	Neither agree nor disagree	Strongly agree

Use the 1-7 numbers to show you agree or disagree.

1. __ I often feel bursts of joy.
2. __ My life is always improving.
3. __ I constantly feel my life is going well.
4. __ I would say that most of the occasions in my life give me joy.
5. __ In a typical day, things often happen that tell me my is working.
6. __ I constantly feel a subtle but enduring feeling of joy.
7. __ I am an intensely cheerful person.
8. __ Many things in my life bring delight.
9. __ I often feel overjoyed when something good happens.
10. __ Even during bad situations, I usually find something to rejoice about.
11. __ I find myself amazed at all the good things I receive.
12. __ I would say I am an enthusiastic person.
13. __ I often feel blessed.

14. __ Good things happen to me all the time.

15. __ I can find joy in most any occasion.

"The present moment is filled with joy. If you are attentive, you will see it."
—Thich Nhat Hanh

Bibliography

Asselin, David. "Christian Maturity and Spiritual Discernment," *Review for Religious*, 27, pp. 581-595, 1968.

Bagozzi, Robert P. "Further Thoughts on the Validity of Measures of Elation, Gladness, and Joy," *Journal of Personality and Social Psychology*, 61, 98-104, 1991.

Barret, Richard. *Liberating the Corporate Soul: Building a Visionary Organization*. Oxford: Butterworth-Heineman, 1998.

Baylor University faculty, staff, and students. Bulletin for worship for the Baylor Religious Hour in advent, 2021.

Bingaman, K.A. "A Pastoral Theological Approach to the New Anxiety," *Pastoral Psychology*, 59, pp. 358-375, 2010.

Bonhoeffer, Dietrich. *The Cost of Discipleship*. New York: The Macmillan Company, 1963.

Bonhoeffer, Dietrich. *Life Together*. New York: Harper & Row, 1952.

Brett, Regina. *Be the Miracle: 50 Lessons for Making the Impossible Possible*. New York: MJF Books, 2012.

Brown, Brené. *Atlas of the Heart*. New York: Random House, 2022.

Buechner, Frederick. *Godric: A Novel*. New York: Harper Collins Publishing Company, 1983.

Capps, David. *Pastoral Counseling and Preaching*. Philadelphia: Westminster Press, 1980.

Chen, Pauline. *Final Exam: A Surgeon's Reflections on Mortality*. New York: Knopf, 2007.

Claypool, John. *Tracks of a Fellow Struggler*. New York: Morehouse Publishers, 1974.

Cox, Harvey. *The Feast of Fools*. New York: Random House, 1965.

D'Arcy, Paula. *Waking Up to This Day: Seeing the Joy Right Before Us*. Maryknoll, New York: Orbis Books, 2009.

De Bottom, Alian. *The School of Life: An Emotional Education*. London: The School of Life Press, 2022.

Edwards, Jonathan. *Religious Affections*, Volume II. New Haven: Yale University Press, 1959.

Eid, Michael, and E. H. Diener, "Norms for Experiencing Emotions in Different Cultures: Inter and International Differences," *Journal of Personality and Social Psychology*, 81, 2001, pp. 869-885.

Ellsworth, Paul, and Carl Smith, "Shades of Joy: Patterns of Appraisal Differentiating Positive Emotions," *Cognitive and Emotion*, 2, pp. 301-312, 2021.

Faukhauser, John. *From a Chicken to an Eagle: What Happens When You Change*. Farmingdale, New York: Coleman Graphics, 1988.

Feingold, A. "Happiness, Unselfishness, and Popularity," *Journal of Psychology*, 115, 1983, pp. 3-5.

Foster, Richard J. *Celebration of Discipline: The Path to Spiritual Growth*. San Francisco: Harper and Row, 1978.

Francis, Holy Father Pope. *Evangelii Gaudium: The Joy of the Gospel*. Boston: Pauline Books, 2013.

Fredrickson, B. I. "What Good Are Positive Emotions?" *Review of General Psychology*, 2, 1998, pp. 300-319.

Fuller, Robert C. *Spiritual but Not Religious: Understanding Unchurched America*. New York: Oxford University Press, 2001.

Goldberg, B.Z. *The Sacred Fire: The Story of Sex in Religion*. New York: University Books, 1958.

Gore, Amanda. *The Gospel of Joy*. Chatswood, Australia: Head to Heart books, 2012.

Hamilton, Adam. *The Lord's Prayer: The Meaning and Power of the Prayer Jesus Taught*. Nashville: Abingdon Press, 2021.

Hauerwas, Stanley. *The Peaceable Kingdom: A Primer in Christian Ethics*. South Bend, Indiana: University of Notre Dame Press, 1983.

Isen, A.M. "Success, Failure, Attention, and Reaction to Others: The Warm Glow of Success," *Journal of Personality and Social Psychology*, 66, 1999, pp. 294-301.

Jones, E. Stanley. *A Song of Ascents: An Autobiography*. Nashville: Abingdon Press, 1968.

Keith, Kent M. *Anyway: The Paradoxical Commandments*. New York: Berkley Publishing Group, 2001.

Kelsey, Morton. *Companions on the Inner Way*. New York: Crossword Books, 1983.

Kierkegaard, Soren. *Purity of Heart Is to Will One Thing: Spiritual Preparation for the Office of Confession*. Trans. Douglas V. Steere. New York: Harper & Row, 1956.

Killinger, John. *A Devotional Guide to Luke: The Gospel of Contagious Joy*. Waco, Texas: Word Books Publisher, 1980.

Killinger, John. *Leave It to the Spirit*. New York: Harper & Row Publishers, 1971.

Killinger, John. *Bread for the Wilderness, Wine for the Journey*. Waco, Texas: Word Books Publisher, 1976.

Killinger, John. *Letting God Bless You: The Beatitudes for Today*. Nashville: Abingdon Press, 1992.

Killinger, John. *Day by Day with Jesus*, Nashville: Abingdon Press, 1994.

Killinger, John. *For God's Sake Be Human*. Waco, Texas: Word Books, Publisher, 1970.

Killinger, John. *Raising Your Spiritual Awareness through 365 Simple Gifts from God*. Nashville: Dimensions for Living, 1998.

Killinger, John. *The Changing Shape of Our Salvation*. New York: Crossroad Publishing House, 2007.

Kushner, Harold. *Living a Life that Matters*. New York: Anchor Books, 2001.

Landis, Kenneth R. and House, J. S. "Social Relationships and Health," *Science*, 241, 1988, pp. 540-545.

Lebo, David, "Some Factors Said to Make for Happiness in Old Age," *Journal of Clinical Psychology*, 9, 1953, pp. 385-387.

Levy, B.R. and S.R. Kunkel, "Longevity Increased by Positive Self-Perceptions of Aging," *Journal of Personality and Social Psychology*, 83, 2002, pp. 261-270.

Lewis, C.S. *Surprised by Joy: The Shape of My Early Life*. New York: Harcourt Brace, 1956.

Lewis, C.S. *The Voyage of the Dawn Treader*. New York: Collier Books 1971.

Lewis, C.S. *The Weight of Glory*. New York: Harper and Collins, 1988.

Lodge, David. *Souls and Bodies*. New York: William Morrow Publishers, 1983.

Lowen, Alexander. *The Betrayal of the Body*. New York: Collier Books, 1967.

Lyubomirsky, S. T., "The Meaning and Expressions of Joy: Comparing the United States and Russia," *American Psychologist*, 56, pp. 239-240.

Linn, E.H. *Preaching as Counseling: The Unique Method of Harry Emerson Fosdick*, Valley Forge, Pennsylvania: Judson Press, 1996.

Macintosh, H. R. *The Originality of the Christian Message: Lectures in Theology*. London: Duckworth Publishers, 1920.

Martin, Curtis. *Making Missionary Disciples: How to Live the Method Modeled by Jesus*. Genesee, Colorado: The Fellowship of Catholic University Students, 2020.

Martin, R. A. "Is Laughter the Best Medicine? Humor, Laughter, and Physical Health," *Current Directions in Psychological Health*, 11, 2002, pp. 216-220.

Marty, Peter W. "Saint Dymphna's Care," The Christian Century, January 2, 2022, p. 3.

McCullough, M.E., and Ron Emmons, "The Grateful Disposition: A Conceptual and Empirical Topology," *Journal of Personality and Social Psychology*, 82, 112127, 2002.

McReynolds, James. Unpublished Doctor of Psychology dissertation, Christ Church College, University of Oxford. *Integration of Joy in Clinical Family Counseling*, 2000.

McReynolds, James. *Joy Comes in the Mourning*. Cleveland, Tennessee: Parson's Porch Books, 2020.

McReynolds, James. *The Joy of Prayer: The Way to Intimacy with God*. Cleveland, Tennessee: Parson's Porch Books, 2020.

McReynolds, James. *The Joy of Preaching: Encountering Jesus through the Word of God*. Cleveland, Tennessee: Parson's Porch Books, 2013.

McReynolds, James. *The Silence of the Church: The Spiritual Struggle with Sexuality*. Cleveland, Tennessee: Parson's Porch Books, 2017.

McReynolds, James. *The Joy of the Kingdom: Envisioning the Great Commission*. Cleveland, Tennessee: Parson's Porch Books, 2020.

McReynolds, James. *The Spirituality of Joy: The Least Discussed Human Emotion*. Cleveland, Tennessee: Parson's Porch Books, 2011.

McReynolds, James. *Visionquest of Joy: The Last Discussed Human Emotion*. Bryn Mawr, Pennsylvania: Dorrance and Company, Incorporated, 1988.

Meyers, David, and Edward Diener, "The Scientific Pursuit of Happiness," *Perspectives on Psychological Science*, 13, number 2, pp. 318-325, 2019.

Miller, R. M. *Harry Emerson Fosdick: Preacher, Pastor, Prophet.* Oxford: Oxford University Press, 1985.

Myers, David G. "Who Is Happy?" *Psychological Science*, 6, 10-19, 2022.

Nelson, Portia. *Autobiography in Five Short Chapters: There's a Hole in My Sidewalk.* New York: Popular Library Publishing, 1978.

Nouwen, Henri. *You Are the Beloved: Daily Meditations for Spiritual Living,* New York: Convergent Books, 2017.

Peck, M. Scott. *People of the Lie: The Hope for Healing Human Evil.* New York: Simon and Schuster, 1986.

Peck, M. Scott. *The Road Less Traveled: A New Psychology of Love.* New York: Simon and Schuster, 1978.

Peterson, Christopher and Martin Seligman, *The Joy and Health Connection,* Harvard Health Publishing. Cambridge: Harvard Medical School, pp. 1-7, 2019.

Plant, Michael. *Doing Good Badly? Philosophical Issues Related to Effective Altruism,"* D.Phil. dissertation, Saint Cross College, University of Oxford, August 2020.

Powers, Isaias. *Quiet Places with Jesus.* Mystic, Connecticut: Twenty-Third Publications, 2012.

Roberts, Robert C. *Spiritual Emotions: A Psychology of Christian Value.* Grand Rapids, Michigan: Eerdmans Publishing, 2007.

James, Ronald. *A Joy Wider Than the World: A Teaching and Preaching Commentary on Philippians.* Nashville: Upper Room Books, 1992.

Reyes-Chow, Bruce. *In Defense of Kindness.* St. Louis, Missouri: Chalice Press, 2022.

Ryan, M.J. *Attitudes of Gratitude: How to Give and Receive Joy Every Day of Your Life.* New York: Conari Press, 2009.

Smith, Karen. "A Baptist Vision of the Church," *Journal of European Baptist Studies,"* pp. 3-23, Prague, Czech Republic: International Baptist Theological Seminary Publications, 2015.

Tillich, Paul. "The Meaning of Joy," *The New Being.* New York: Charles Scribner and Sons, 1965.

Tillich, Paul. *Systematic Theology, Volume One.* Chicago: University of Chicago Press, 1951.

Tompkins, Steven. *Affect, Imagery, and Consciousness.* New York: Springer Press, 1999.

Underhill, Evelyn. *A Study of the Nature and Development in Human Consciousness.* New York: The New American Library Incorporated, 1955.

Van deWalle, Janet. "Kindness," *Women's Edition.* Omaha: Business Press, January 2022, p. 38.

Von Hildebrand, *Love Refined: Letters to a Young Bride.* Manchester, New Hampshire: Sophia Institute Press, 1989.

Van Kaam, Adrian. *The Roots of Christian Joy.* Denville, New Jersey: Dimension Books, 1988.

Walker, Williston. *A History of the Christian Church.* New York: Charles Scribner's Sons, 1970.

Watkins, P.C. and Kenneth Woodward, Thomas Stone, and Robert Kolts, "Gratitude and Happiness: Development of a Measure of Gratitude, and Relationships with Subjective Well-being," *Social Behavior and Personality: An International Journal,* 31, 431-451.

Watkins, P.C., *Favors from Heaven: Source and Benefits of Gratitude Toward God.* San Diego: American Psychological Association, 2010.

Watson, Christie. *The Language of Kindness: A Nurse's Story*. New York: Tim Duggan Books, 2021.

Wells, Donald A., "Words for Grief," *The Christian Century*, 139, 5, March 9, 2022, p.6

Wilber, Kay. *Eye to Eye: The Quest for a New Paradigm*. Garden City, New York: Doubleday, 1987.

Williams, S.D. *The Practice of Personal Transformation*. Berkeley, California: Journey Press, 1985.

Wimberley, E. M. *Moving from Shame to Self-Worth: Preaching and Pastoral Care*. Nashville: Abingdon Press, 2000.

Woititz, J. G. *Struggle for Intimacy*. Pompano Beach, Florida: Health Communications, 1988.

Woolman, *The Journal of John Wolman*. Secaucus, New York: The Citadel Press, 1972.

Wordsworth, William. *Surprised by Joy and Other Poems*. New York: Knopf Publishers, 1995.

About the Author

James McReynolds celebrates 70 years of ministry in 2023. He has served as a preacher, teacher, therapist, and writer. He has devoted his more than 80 years of life communicating how to create an atmosphere for joy and miracles.

Millions have read his books, articles, and printed sermons. Others have listened to Jim's radio and television presentations. As a licensed psychotherapist, he deeply believes that souls are made for endurance. McReynolds' long ministry has revolutionized the lives of countless people.

Norman Vincent Peale, famous preacher of positive thinking at Marble Collegiate Church in New York, anointed Jim the Minister of Joy to the World.

McReynolds believes his world travels are miracles from God. Parson's Porch has been the publisher of 13 of his last books that have mysteriously reached people in places only miracles could provide. Agnes Hull, Jim's English professor at Carson Newman, got him in touch with Charles Trentham, pastor, First Baptist Church in Knoxville, Tennessee. He served that church as student minister of prayer during his years as a student.

Opportunities to serve always come as a complete joyous surprise such as service as a public relations specialist for the Sunday School Board of the Southern Baptist Convention. Harold Bales, a close friend and fellow student at Vanderbilt
University Divinity School, served in much the same capacity at the Methodist
Board of Evangelism. Bales' deep friendship led McReynolds' to serve United Methodist congregations where he became an ordained deacon and finally an elder in the Holston Conference.

While serving the First Christian Church in Polo and Kingston Christian Church in Kingston, Missouri, he received a call as pastor of the Zion United Church of Christ in Saint Joseph, Missouri known for their massive organ, a gymnasium, perfect acoustics, and a television ministry. Jim read scripture from the German to show respect and kindness to the people who belonged to the Evangelical and Reformed Church. Former pastors preached in the

German language. The lovely downtown church was another miracle. McReynolds is a retired elder in full membership connection in the Holston Conference of the United Methodist Church.

Jim's final United Methodist appointment was in his hometown, Saint Luke United Methodist Church was in Bristol, Virginia-Tennessee. Jim and his wife Laurel moved to Nebraska where he got a quick calling to the First Christian Church in Pawnee City. He served several churches before accepting a call from the First Christian Church in Weeping Water where he served for nearly 11 years.

Jim is active in the ministry of the Nebraska Region of the Christian Church (Disciples of Christ) where he was surprised to be elected the moderator of the regional board.

Contact the author at 320 North Fourth Street, Elmwood, NE 68349. His email is joyminister@windstream.net.

His website is jamesevansmcreynolds.com.

His phone number is 402-994-2370.

Other Books by James McReynolds

The Spirituality of Joy: The Least Discussed Human Emotion

The Joy of Preaching: Encountering Jesus through the Word of God

Dancing with God: A Theology of Joy

The Silence of the Church: The Spiritual Struggle with Sexuality

The Spirit of Joy Church

Joy Comes in the Mourning: Love Is Forever

The Joy of Prayer

Envisioning the Great Commission: The Joy of the Kingdom

Walking in the Garden with God

Joy in the Seasons of Life

Living the Dream: Amazing Adventure in Marriage

Joy Beyond the Walls of This World: Healing the Souls of Men and Women

The Gospel of Joy: Global Impact of the Ministry of Joy to the World

www.ingramcontent.com/pod-product-compliance
Lightning Source LLC
Chambersburg PA
CBHW071009120626
46546CB00003B/999